# Television Today and Tomorrow

# Television Today and Tomorrow

## It Won't Be What You Think

Gene F. Jankowski

David C. Fuchs

New York   Oxford
OXFORD UNIVERSITY PRESS     1995

Oxford University Press

Oxford    New York
Athens    Auckland    Bangkok    Bombay
Calcutta    Cape Town    Dar es Salaam    Delhi
Florence    Hong Kong    Istanbul    Karachi
Kuala Lumpur    Madras    Madrid    Melbourne
Mexico City    Nairobi    Paris    Singapore
Taipei    Tokyo    Toronto

and associated companies in
Berlin    Ibadan

Copyright © 1995 by Oxford University Press, Inc.

Published by Oxford University Press, Inc.
200 Madison Avenue, New York, New York 10016

Oxford is a registered trademark of Oxford University Press

Library of Congress Cataloging-in-Publication Data
Jankowski, Gene F.
Television today and tomorrow :
it won't be what you think
by Gene F. Jankowski and David C. Fuchs.
p.   cm. Includes bibliographical references and index.
ISBN 0–19–507487–4
1. Television broadcasting—United States.
2. Television programs—United States.
3. Television broadcasting of news—United States.
I. Fuchs, David C.   II. Title. PN1992.3.U5J36
1995   791.45'0973—dc20    94-26778

1 2 3 4 5 6 7 8 9

Printed in the United States of America
on acid-free paper

# Preface

Between 1927 and 1995, the American people went from listening to crystal radio sets with a few miles' range to watching television programs in color that arrive instantaneously from any part of the world. Cable has multiplied the choices of programs in a way unimaginable even a generation ago. The experts tell us that we will soon be wired to an information superhighway—bringing even more choices of both programs and interactive connections to a world of goods and games.

What will all of this mean for the networks that were the engine of the phenomenal growth of television into the powerful medium it has become? Will they become just one more choice among hundreds, no longer able to attract the millions of dollars in advertising that fuels their popular programming? Or will they, as many have warned, become extinct, like the dinosaurs, unable to survive in the flood of competing channels?

We think, contrary to current wisdom, that they will continue to thrive! This book explains why we believe this. It also provides an opportunity to look at the current state of television—with a special focus on the way the networks work—and argue that the future landscape of television may not be what many people expect.

We realize that our view is probably a minority opinion. Many, perhaps most, of the readers will not agree with what we have to say. We do hope, however, to encourage further thinking about the nature of the most pervasive medium the world has ever known.

To understand where television is today and where it will be tomorrow, it is necessary to know something about the origins of broadcasting. Television grew out of the networks that were created at the dawn of radio. It is the result of more than sixty years of invention, experimentation, and commerce. It was forged by a combination of risk takers, entrepreneurs, creative geniuses, and financial wizards. We therefore begin our book with a brief look at this evolution.

We then describe the creative process by which programs are created and how it affects the programs we see. Central to any understanding of television is knowing where the money comes from, and we explain the role of advertisers in bringing programs to viewers. We show how government regulations—now in the process of undergoing significant changes—determine who profits the most from program production and what effect this has on the end product. And, of course, we face up to the critics of television, who often seem to us to have a tenuous grasp of the realities of the business. Finally, we look into the future and see a different picture from that of many others.

Our credentials for writing this book are that we witnessed firsthand much of the recent history of television. Together we spent a total of sixty-three years at CBS in a variety of jobs that taught us how the networks really work.

The book itself grew out of a course that Jankowski taught at Michigan State University. Several of the professors suggested that a book about the television industry written by those who lived it might provide a very useful perspective. We took the suggestion, and this book is the result. We hope that it contributes to an understanding of this most fascinating and often misunderstood medium.

*New York*                                    G. F. J.
*Lloyd Harbor, N.Y.*                           D. C. F.
*June 1994*

# Acknowledgments

During our years at CBS we had the privilege of working with, observing, and learning from many talented colleagues and associates in all parts of the creative, distribution, and funding areas.

They include Don Hewitt, the executive producer of *60 Minutes* for all its twenty-five years; Norman Lear, the man behind many successful situation comedies, such as *All in the Family* and *Sanford and Son;* Lee Rich, who gave CBS some of its most successful shows during the 1970s and 1980s—*The Waltons, Falcon Crest, Knots Landing,* and *Dallas,* one episode of which received the second-highest rating in the history of network television (53.3), surpassed only by the final episode of *M\*A\*S\*H* (60.3); William Paley, founder of CBS in 1927, and with whom Gene had the opportunity to discuss the business, one-on-one, for more than eleven years; Frank Stanton, president of CBS for thirty-five years and the one, perhaps more than anyone, responsible for the CBS image of quality and integrity; Bill Leonard, a multifaceted executive experienced as an on-air broadcaster, news producer, and former president of CBS News; Tom Chauncey, former owner of one of the CBS network's best affiliates, who attributed his success to "just clearing everything CBS sends me"; Red Martin, affiliate owner, engineer, broadcast pioneer, and truly a wise and observing man; Augie Meyer, owner of more than one station and broadcast pioneer, who understood the value of community service and maintaining strong Washington connections; Arch Madsen, retired executive of Bonneville Broadcasting, another of the pioneers of the industry, who knew the importance of quality programming; Perry Wolff, writer and producer of many CBS News documentaries and winner of fourteen Peabody Awards and six Emmys; Arthur Godfrey, radio and TV performer, who understood the power of the audience and the power of the medium as a sales tool; Bob Daly, former president of CBS Entertainment and current chairman of Warner Brothers Pictures; Lou Dorfsman, an award-winning art director/designer who set high standards for advertising programs and for promoting a company image; Walter Cronkite, who worked to defend the integrity of CBS News both as a member of the CBS Board of Directors and as an anchorman; and Dan Rather, who had the very difficult task of replacing "the most trusted man in America," and who has demonstrated for more than a decade that he is quite capable of doing so.

And no discourse about network television would be complete without some reference to the very talented and dedicated technicians and engineers whose pride and devotion keep the programs flowing over the airwaves day after day, week after week, year after year. With the very rarest of exceptions, the television screens have not "gone black" during the normal broadcast day in more than thirty-five years thanks to thousands of these special people, most of whom belong to the crafts and trade unions. To name them all is not possible; to name one to be emblematic for them all is a pleasure: George Naeder, a network cameraman for more than forty years, whose tough exterior during union negotiations belied a warm and caring heart almost as big as he was.

These are just a handful of the many people who, along

with dozens of talented executives, have helped to enrich our lives. We have also been rewarded as viewers, since many of their activities also helped to enrich the screen.

Finally, this book is the result of the input of many friends and colleagues. To Professors Tom Muth, Brad Greenberg, and Tom Baldwin of Michigan State University for their encouragement to write a book about television as seen through the eyes of two people who experienced it and had a role in influencing the process and procedures, a special thank-you.

There are also a number of people from whom we requested ideas about what television might be like after the year 2000. For Carl Lee, Dan Rather, Fred Silverman, Thomas Murphy, Bill Moyers, Leonard Goldenson, Red Martin, Charles Crutchfield, Walter Cronkite, Mike Wallace, Richard Wiley, Don Hewitt, Harvey Shepherd, Homer Lane, Newton Minow, Ed Bliss, and Ward Quaal, who took time out of their busy schedules to respond thoughtfully, we have the deepest gratitude.

Any project of this sort requires timely comments from knowledgeable individuals. We are most appreciative to Phil Harding, for many years a very knowledgeable and highly respected social research expert at CBS; Jack Blessington, educator and CBS colleague; David Poltrack and Michael Eisenberg of CBS research; David Wilkofsky of Wilkofsky-Gruen; Judy Jankowski, and Carole Suarez. All these thoughtful people provided us with helpful observations and suggestions. And finally, we thank our families for their support and understanding over the years, especially when unscheduled events disrupted our lives.

# Contents

Introduction    3

1. A Brief History of Broadcasting    9
2. The Creative Product    27
3. Where the Money Comes From    49
4. Television and Washington    97
5. Television and Its Critics    121
6. The Future    153

Postscript: A Failed Takeover Attempt    213
Glossary    223
Bibliography    227
Index    233

# Television Today and Tomorrow

# Introduction

In this book we examine certain aspects of the way constantly advancing developments in communications technology have interacted with the lives, habits, needs, and interests of the American people in the past, and how the two are apt to be related in the future. Our particular focus is on television.

At this time, billions of dollars are being invested, and vast new alliances are being formed involving telephone companies, cable systems, computer businesses, publishers, and motion picture studios in the belief that the future of communications is to be found in the conjunction of the telephone, the television set, and the computer.

The expectation is that all of the services these organizations now offer separately will be combined in a single appliance that will be a movie theater, stereo, printer, telephone, mailbox, library, classroom, playroom, diary, checkbook, calendar, television screen, or any combination of these.

Unlike its predecessors, the new appliance will be alert, able to receive and execute commands and carry out instructions, and capable of remembering and reminding, calculating, storing, and retrieving. Companies are now positioning themselves to compete for a share of an immense, unified electronic market of the future.

The technology to achieve this clearly is, or will be, available. What is not so clear is whether the customers will be. At issue is the way in which people order their lives. The basis for the view that we will all eventually participate in this new market in the future is the enormous success of television in the past. All sorts of new uses are to be grafted on to this existing main stem. The attraction is that the customer is already there. It is a simple matter to add to the options. We believe a careful reading of television's history suggests that this is not so easily done. The race does not necessarily go to the newest and fastest, as an interesting case-in-point illustrates.

The story begins with a clumsy rig that gave people with poor reception a better picture. It was known as CATV, Community Antenna Television. And that's exactly what it was— one big antenna replacing a lot of small ones, bringing in the local stations and maybe some not quite local, too.

People were willing to pay for it. That did not mean much until satellites made it possible to put other kinds of programs on it. HBO was born. CNN was born. Showtime was born. WTBS, The Superstation, was born. Then they came in batches—ESPN, The Discovery Channel, The Disney Channel, FNN, Lifetime, MTV, Nickelodeon, TNT, Nashville, Arts & Entertainment, The Learning Channel, The American Movie Channel, The Weather Channel, USA, The Home Shopping Channel, QVC. And on it goes.

What had been three choices became ten, twenty, fifty, with one hundred and even five hundred promised down the road, along with a marriage between the video tube and the computer screen that would deliver to the living room what all the libraries, newspapers, magazines, movies, books, laboratories, art galleries, museums, universities, theaters, sports arenas, stock exchanges, parliaments, and town halls in the world produced.

What would be the fate of the three old dowagers of the business—the networks—with all this happening? The answer seemed obvious: they were doomed. Yet, amid all of the exuberant stories about the possibilities of the new technologies, the most telling development was in the old one. In 1987, an Australian newspaperman, Rupert Murdoch, decided to launch a new network, but not on cable. Instead, he put together a string of old-fashioned, independent television stations, none of them even leaders in their markets. He began by offering eight hours of prime-time programming each week.

He was out of step. This was the method of the 1920s and '30s, the way ABC, CBS, and NBC were born, when there was no cable competition. Not only was it very expensive, but he didn't even have the advantage cable systems get from carrying all three networks' programs at no cost to them.

Murdoch went ahead. By 1990 he had a larger audience than any one of the new cable services. By 1993 it was larger than any five of them. Why this happened, and what it means in five-hundred-channel future, is what this book is about.

We are aware of the reasons that proponents of the new technological developments feel as they do. Their enthusiasm is understandable. What is not so often mentioned are the harsh business facts behind their strategies. The cable companies fear the entry of deregulated phone companies into their business, and the phone companies fear the entry of deregulated cable companies into theirs. Both have also reached the limits of market penetration. Because they cannot grow by adding more customers, they will have to grow by getting more from the customers they have. This can be done only by adding new services. As for the computer companies, replacement of the television set by the telecomputer means both a hardware and a software bonanza. So a vast, new, unified electronic marketplace would present enormous opportunities for each of them.

The motivations of these companies are clear, but we believe that not enough attention has been paid to the motivations of their presumed customers, and a key to that is to be found in the reasons networks continue to succeed in a world of constantly expanding competition. Multibillion-dollar bets are being placed on new technological developments, on the basis of highly questionable assumptions. If our reading of the market is correct, many of these wagers will be lost.

As a basis for our position, in the next chapter we provide a very brief history of television. We do not offer this chapter as a complete textbook. There are many of those. This is the story of the underlying and still applicable network business dynamic. The next chapter may also prove to be a helpful primer for those without any previous knowledge of the early development of the networks.

Chapter *1*

# A Brief History of Broadcasting

There never has been a personality as dominant in the industry as Arthur Godfrey was in the 1950s and '60s. He had two TV shows in the top ten as well as a two-hour weekday program carried on both radio and television. Gene once received an opportunity to fly to Buffalo with Godfrey, an expert pilot who flew his own plane everywhere. On the way back, after Godfrey had finished charming the local citizens, Gene noticed a pattern in the radio conversation as they flew in and out of various flight control sectors. It went like this: "Rochester, this is Mike One at five thousand feet." "Right, Mike One, you're clear." "Thanks Rochester." "Good night, Mister Godfrey." Every single air traffic controller knew that Mike One was Arthur Godfrey. Gene asked him how this could be. "Every Christmas," he said, "I send out thousands of grease pencils to the controllers—that's how they mark their radar scopes—with a note of appreciation signed 'From you friend, Arthur Godfrey.'" It was a perfect illustration of Godfrey the performer and Godfrey the salesman, the one interchangeable with the other. Nobody in the business ever combined the two roles as successfully as he did. And there was a lesson in that. American broadcasting is a marriage—not just a passing acquaintance—between art and commerce. The business can be fully understood only if the nature of that relationship is fully understood.

Godfrey, like Jack Benny, Bob Hope, Red Skelton, and Jack Paar, was one of the great transitional figures in broadcasting, a radio star who moved triumphantly into television. This was not always the case. Radio as a performers' medium was radically different from television. Many other stars and formats did not transfer successfully. In an experiential sense, radio did not prepare the way for television; nothing did. And yet radio, the business, did prepare the way for television, the business. This has important implications for the industry as it exists today.

The audience, however, was not interested in the business behind the tube. When television arrived, they could not believe their eyes. The thing they went to the movie houses for, images that moved and spoke, suddenly came to them. All the massive technology of motion pictures—the resplendent theaters, the huge, dark interiors, the cone of brilliant light stabbing out of a booth above their heads—was now contained in an invisible beam that penetrated the walls and emerged right in their living rooms. They crowded outside appliance store windows and gathered in neighbors' homes to stare at the new miracle. The program quality by today's standards was often primitive, but the experience was not. That sense of novelty is now gone forever, because the innocence that produced it is gone, but it is impossible to underestimate the intoxicating power of the new medium.

There is more to this than remembering stories of the past. There is also a business issue to be considered. To understand how television works today, it is necessary to understand its beginnings. Even in the business sense, 'the past is prologue.' Television became a viable business rapidly because it was built on top of a viable business, radio, that had the systems it

Arthur Godfrey, talented radio and television personality, delivered sponsors' commercials in addition to being the star of his own programs.
*Source:* CBS Inc.

needed. Television ultimately took over the mass medium functions of radio. In the 1980s, the new technologies of cable, satellites, and VCRs were simply added to television as it was. Rather than replacing it, they built out from its margins.

From the earliest stages, the government had a role in the development of radio. The military needs of World War I had greatly accelerated radio technology. Smaller and simpler sets were produced for wartime use. Soon, all over America, entrepreneurs with a knack for gadgets were going on the air, often interfering with each other's signals. Finally the government had to be called in to restore order. Frequencies were licensed, one to a customer. Thus government regulation began as an engineering issue.

It was not long before station owners discovered that a station operating alone rarely had the resources to produce enough attractive programming to hold on to an audience and the advertising that came with it. That's how networks came about. The idea was that a big enough distribution system—produced by connecting stations to each other—could attract enough advertising money to support better programming. The radio networks and the individual stations that composed them gradually worked out a time-sharing arrangement whereby part of the day was set aside for local programming provided by each station and part for network programs carried by all the stations. That system of interlocking national and local programming was, and is, unique to broadcasting in America.

In the process, radio broadcasters learned a great deal about what the public wanted. Well before television, radio broadcasters had had to monitor the public's taste. That was one piece of the foundation upon which television was able to build. Another was the advertisers who had sponsored programs on radio. They were ready-made candidates for investing in television. Their advertising agencies knew how to produce and place commercials, and programs as well. There was an established corps of talent trained to the demands of a live electronic medium. Even the buildings from the older medium became the foundations of the new one. Finally, there was a huge audience already in place.

Thus, the social patterns, as well as the basic business cycle that would sustain television, were already in place when the first flickering images came into the home. The transition from radio to television was not one of system, but of scale. Sight, sound, and motion were far more difficult to handle than sound alone. A car chase on the radio was handled by a sound effects expert producing squealing tires and the roar of engines. On television real cars with real drivers on real streets were needed, plus cameras and a crew to film them, followed by film laboratories and workrooms equipped and staffed for the required post-production work. Television was far more costly, but it was also far more effective, which meant that advertisers were willing to pay the higher prices.

The programs might have had a touch of magic about them—all creative enterprises do—but the system itself would have been familiar to any businessperson. There had to be a means of developing product, a kind of laboratory where new ideas could be tried out. There had to be a means of producing

A radio drama being conducted by Orson Welles and starring the Mercury Playhouse performers.
*Source:* Welles Family

what came out of the laboratory. There had to be a means of distributing that product, getting it to the consumer. Finally, there had to be a means of paying for the development, the production, and the distribution. And each of these parts had to be ongoing. They could not be set up independently every time a new production was under consideration. Broadcasting was a continuous medium. Hour after hour, day after day, time had to be filled. It would grow into a theater that would never be dark, never be empty. There had never been a creative challenge quite like it. To this day, there is no other medium that has a creative challenge as difficult as that of television. Meeting this challenge demanded systematization.

The requirements were self-evident. The hidden ingredi- ent—the thing that had been worked out gradually in radio as the medium grew—was not any one of these things, but rather the relationship among them. They had to fit together. There was no point in attempting to develop a product that the distribution system would not accept, or one whose production costs were insupportable, or one for which there was no demand. So the needs, the capacities, and the skills of one part of the cycle had to be known to, and accommodated by, the other parts.

This fit did not happen all by itself. There is an intense rivalry, sometimes bordering on paranoia, among these industry segments. Distributors think producers are crazy; producers think distributors are boring; both are convinced they are being exploited by the other. It is not unusual to have serious court actions between them even while they are doing business with each other. Indeed, intra-segment rivalry is a prime mover behind much of the regulatory structure of the medium. Even at this time, the networks, cable, independent stations, and the production community are all engaged in rival claims for more, or less, regulation in each of their spheres.

It was radio that learned how to fit these pieces together. The price of that success was countless experiments and lots of failures. Success is often nothing more than the gradual elimination of mistakes. It is easy to describe the theory, but it was not theory that built transmitters, wrote scripts, and sold advertising time. It was trial and error, full of stories like this one: "With all that signal, we installed studios in the Herpolsheimer store in Grand Rapids, expecting to get some of the Grand Rapids market, but after three years we never garnered more than a 10 or 12 share. It just wasn't enough to do local business in Grand Rapids."

The speaker above is Carl Lee, who was the engineer at the station with "all that signal"—WKZO radio in Kalamazoo, owned by John Fetzer, one of the pioneers in broadcasting. WKZO was trying to get a foothold in Grand Rapids, fifty miles from home base. So they beefed up the signal and built a studio in the biggest store in town. The idea was to do local programming and build up a local following. But it didn't work. Grand Rapids was unimpressed. Eventually Carl Lee and John Fetzer's company did make it there, but not until they got a license and built a new station in Grand Rapids.

That's how broadcasting grew in America: one station at a time, one town at a time, incrementally, like a coral reef. It is impossible to understand the system as it is today without understanding this step-by-step process. The networks were also built from the ground up, lining up affiliates like WKZO, lining up talent, lining up sponsors, putting shows on the air, and finding out who listened. Each part of the cycle pushed the other forward—extending distribution, extending production, extending funding by extending audience.

It was not for another forty years that this step-by-step process was superseded, when cable increased the means of distribution by geometric leaps without a matching growth in production. What that led to will be treated later.

## The Networks and the Age of Production

Television inherited a mature production, distribution and funding system from radio. That is why the years from 1950 through 1975 were ones of uninterrupted growth. CBS and NBC were the major players. ABC was an enterprising, but distant, third, a not-quite-equal competitor with lesser resources, but a contributor of energy, ideas, and product. The networks paid a price for this success. By the late '60s and early '70s, they were being perceived as a kind of unelected second government. Many in Washington felt they had to be reined in. In the early 1970s, several restrictions were imposed on them.

The Prime Time Access Rule limited the amount of time stations in the top fifty cities could carry network programs to three hours, between six and eleven o'clock each night, seven days a week. A fourth hour on Sunday could also be programmed, provided it was a documentary or a public affairs or children's program—a provision that came to be very liberally interpreted. The law also stipulated that network affiliates in

In the early days of television, most programs were live, such as Ed Sullivan's "Toast of the Town."
*Source:* Andrew Salt Productions

the fifty largest markets could not purchase reruns of network programs for local use. Although this part of the rule appears to be a clear infringement of a station's First Amendment rights, it was not challenged seriously until 1993, when the Disney Corporation began to take steps to have it changed. One reason for the relative lack of activity is that the major segments of the industry—networks, stations, Hollywood producers, and major studios—do not share the same opinion with regard to its value. Even so, by the fall of 1994 the FCC said that the rule would be revised, with the belief that it would eventually be eliminated.

The Financial Interest and Syndication Rule eliminated the networks' ability to partially own or invest in programs produced by others. The only programs the networks could own were those produced by the network itself. Program ownership was further controlled by the consent decrees the networks had with the Department of Justice. The decrees dictated the number of hours that network-owned entertainment programs could be broadcast each week. Network news and sports programs were exempt from this law. And networks were barred from owning cable systems. Even so, from the early '50s through the '70s, the networks had the field to themselves. They competed only with each other, and they had nearly 90 percent of the audience. By November 1985, these rules, too, would seem set.

## Cable and the Age of Distribution

The restrictions placed on the networks had been justified by the legislators on the grounds of distribution scarcity. Scarcity meant that since there were only three networks, there was limited choice. The deregulation of cable was intended to remedy this situation, and it did. Distribution scarcity soon became distribution excess. This was the main result of what is often referred to as the "era of the new technologies." The most important of these were the VCR—in a sense, an unlimited channel—and the combination of satellites and cable. What deregulation would eventually lead to was a radical imbalance between production and distribution whose effects are only now beginning to be felt.

While VCRs and cable were the distinguishing factors of the '80s, they did not have the expected result. They did not displace the networks or even compete with them directly. In fact, by far the largest use of VCRs was, and is, recorded playback of network programs. But they did affect the networks.

Excluding the networks from cable was one thing; the growth of cable was another. Cable's selling point was a clearer picture. It retransmitted the signals of the broadcast stations. Its most popular fare and main source of revenue was the networks' programming. This meant that the networks' product was fueling the growth of its competitors. As well as adding new channels in its own right, cable also expanded the coverage areas of UHF stations. This greatly enlarged the demand for syndicated programming—that is, the programming sold individually to stations. The networks found themselves regulated out of what became a multibillion-dollar market largely consisting of programming they had originally paid for and popularized. Still, for their own survival, they had to continue to invest in the product that would eventually become their competitor, and at ever-increasing costs.

Looking at the situation that developed, it was easy to conclude that the networks were dinosaurs—evolutionary misfits doomed to extinction. It seemed simple: they had gotten fat when the three of them had the whole feeding ground to themselves. How could they survive when fifty new competitors came along? From the '80s onward, a favorite theme of media analysts was the inevitable demise of the networks. For instance, the cover story of the August 19, 1979, edition of the *New York Times Magazine* was titled "Television Enters the 80's." It contained this line: "The kind of storm that swept Dorothy off to Oz is about to hit the old Broadcasting industry."

By "old Broadcasting industry," it meant the networks. The wiring of the nation was proceeding rapidly, and with cable came multiple channels. New forms of over-the-air transmission were also on the horizon. Videodiscs and video cassettes were coming into the marketplace; low-power television stations were about to be built; the number of independent stations was growing; and the superstation had made its appearance. The networks' share did in fact decline, but the rest of the story was different: the networks did not disappear, and many of the new viewing choices are having a tougher time surviving than the old ones. Let's review why this assessment turned out to be wrong.

To begin with the business side, many observers misunderstood the meaning of the term *share* to the networks. They forgot that shares have been declining since the second television station went on the air. They did not realize that share was never the controlling fact in the business life of the networks. What advertisers buy is circulation, not share. As shown in Tables 1–1 and 1–2, in spite of all the new competition, in 1992 the networks reached almost the same size audience they had reached in 1980 and a larger audience than they had reached in the 1970s. And those audiences were still larger, by far, than those available through any other source.

## Two Kinds of Needs

Behind these miscalculations is a misunderstanding of the nature of the needs the networks fill and the nature of the needs people have.

Almost any newsstand or library reveals that, broadly speaking, each of us has two kinds of communications needs. One has to do with shared interests. In information, this means we want to keep in touch with what is going on in our community, our state, our country, and the world in general. In terms of entertainment, our need is expressed in the common human fondness for sharing a good joke or a good story or a good tune. This need is the underpinning of the popular arts—listening to the hit songs, reading best-sellers, going to the most popular movies, watching favorite television shows.

The networks' success in meeting these shared interests was often disparaged. It was said to be based on nothing more than lack of competition. Therefore, they would not survive in a multichannel world. But that did not happen, for at least two reasons. The first is that the success of the networks was no accident. With fifty years of experience, an excellent system for measuring audience responses, and the resources to handle almost every known entertainment and informational form, the networks knew what they were doing. The second is that

TABLE 1-1.

| Program | Net | Season | Rank | Rtg. | Share |
|---|---|---|---|---|---|
| *HUT = 10,970,000* | | | | | |
| Texaco Star Theater (6,757,200) | NBC | 1950–51 | 1 | 61.6 | 81 |
| Fireside Theater | NBC | 1950–51 | 2 | 52.6 | 72 |
| Philco TV Playhouse | NBC | 1950–51 | 3 | 45.3 | 66 |
| Your Show of Shows | NBC | 1950–51 | 4 | 42.6 | 63 |
| Colgate comedy Hour, The | NBC | 1950–51 | 5 | 42.0 | 57 |
| Gillette Cavalcade of Sports | NBC | 1950–51 | 6 | 41.3 | 60 |
| Lone Ranger, The | ABC | 1950–51 | 7 | 41.2 | 64 |
| Arthur Godfrey's Talent Scouts | CBS | 1950–51 | 8 | 40.6 | 56 |
| Hopalong Cassidy | NBC | 1950–51 | 9 | 39.9 | 74 |
| Mama | CBS | 1950–51 | 10 | 39.7 | 57 |
| Robert Montgomery Presents | NBC | 1950–51 | 11 | 38.8 | 54 |
| Martin Kane, Private Eye | NBC | 1950–51 | 12 | 37.8 | 59 |
| Man Against Crime | CBS | 1950–51 | 13 | 37.4 | 56 |
| Kraft Television Theater | NBC | 1950–51 | 14 | 37.0 | 52 |
| Toast of the Town | CBS | 1950–51 | 15 | 36.5 | 51 |
| Aldrich Family, The | NBC | 1950–51 | 16 | 36.1 | 52 |
| You Bet Your Life | NBC | 1950–51 | 17 | 36.0 | 53 |
| Arthur Godfrey and His Friends | CBS | 1950–51 | 18 | 35.9 | 51 |
| Armstrong Circle Theater | NBC | 1950–51 | 19 | 35.6 | 52 |
| Big Town | CBS | 1950–51 | 20 | 35.6 | 51 |
| | | | | | |
| *HUT = 46,330,000* | | | | | |
| Gunsmoke (17,281,000) | CBS | 1960–61 | 1 | 37.3 | 62 |
| Wagon Train | NBC | 1960–61 | 2 | 34.2 | 55 |
| Have Gun Will Travel | CBS | 1960–61 | 3 | 30.9 | 49 |
| Andy Griffith Show, The | CBS | 1960–61 | 4 | 27.8 | 44 |
| Real McCoys, The | ABC | 1960–61 | 5 | 27.7 | 43 |
| Rawhide | CBS | 1960–61 | 6 | 27.5 | 47 |
| Candid Camera | CBS | 1960–61 | 7 | 27.3 | 46 |
| Untouchables, he | ABC | 1960–61 | 8 | 27.0 | 44 |
| Price Is Right, The | NBC | 1960–61 | 9 | 27.0 | 41 |
| Jack Benny Show, The | CBS | 1960–61 | 10 | 26.2 | 42 |
| Dennis the Menace | CBS | 1960–61 | 11 | 26.1 | 42 |
| Danny Thomas Show, The | CBS | 1960–61 | 12 | 25.9 | 39 |
| 77 Sunset Strip | ABC | 1960–61 | 13 | 25.8 | 42 |
| My Three Sons | ABC | 1960–61 | 14 | 25.8 | 40 |
| Ed Sullivan Show, The | CBS | 1960–61 | 15 | 25.0 | 38 |
| Perry Mason | CBS | 1960–61 | 16 | 24.9 | 39 |
| Bonanza | NBC | 1960–61 | 17 | 24.8 | 39 |
| Flintstones, The | ABC | 1960–61 | 18 | 24.3 | 39 |

TABLE 1–1. (Continued)

| Program | Net | Season | Rank | Rtg. | Share |
|---|---|---|---|---|---|
| Red Skelton Show, The | CBS | 1960–61 | 19 | 24.0 | 38 |
| General Electric Theater | CBS | 1960–61 | 20 | 23.4 | 36 |
| *HUT = 60,100,000* | | | | | |
| Marcus Welby, M.D. (17,789,600) | ABC | 1970–71 | 1 | 29.6 | 52 |
| Flip Wilson Show, The | NBC | 1970–71 | 2 | 27.9 | 43 |
| Here's Lucy | CBS | 1970–71 | 3 | 26.1 | 38 |
| Ironside | NBC | 1970–71 | 4 | 25.7 | 39 |
| Gunsmoke | CBS | 1970–71 | 5 | 25.5 | 39 |
| ABC Movie of the Week | ABC | 1970–71 | 6 | 25.1 | 38 |
| Hawaii Five-O | CBS | 1970–71 | 7 | 25.0 | 44 |
| Medical Center | CBS | 1970–71 | 8 | 24.5 | 37 |
| Bonanza | NBC | 1970–71 | 9 | 23.9 | 36 |
| F.B.I., The | ABC | 1970–71 | 10 | 23.0 | 35 |
| Mod Squad, The | ABC | 1970–71 | 11 | 22.7 | 35 |
| Adam 12 | NBC | 1970–71 | 12 | 22.6 | 36 |
| Wonderful World of Disney, The | NBC | 1970–71 | 13 | 22.4 | 35 |
| Rowan & Martin's Laugh-In | NBC | 1970–71 | 14 | 22.4 | 33 |
| Mayberry R.F.D. | CBS | 1970–71 | 15 | 22.3 | 33 |
| Hee Haw | CBS | 1970–71 | 16 | 21.4 | 32 |
| Mannix | CBS | 1970–71 | 17 | 21.3 | 38 |
| Men From Shiloh, The | NBC | 1970–71 | 18 | 21.2 | 33 |
| My Three Sons | CBS | 1970–71 | 19 | 20.8 | 34 |
| Doris Day Show, The | CBS | 1970–71 | 20 | 20.7 | 31 |
| *HUT = 79,900,000* | | | | | |
| Dallas (27,565,000) | CBS | 1980–81 | 1 | 33.4 | 55 |
| 60 Minutes | CBS | 1980–81 | 2 | 27.8 | 43 |
| Dukes of Hazzard, The | CBS | 1980–81 | 3 | 26.3 | 42 |
| M*A*S*H | CBS | 1980–81 | 4 | 24.8 | 35 |
| Love Boat, The | ABC | 1980–81 | 5 | 24.3 | 41 |
| Private Benjamin | CBS | 1980–81 | 6 | 23.9 | 37 |
| Jeffersons, The | CBS | 1980–81 | 7 | 23.4 | 35 |
| Alice | CBS | 1980–81 | 8 | 22.8 | 33 |
| NBC Tuesday Night at the Movies | NBC | 1980–81 | 9 | 22.6 | 33 |
| Three's Company | ABC | 1980–81 | 10 | 22.4 | 33 |
| House Calls | CBS | 1980–81 | 11 | 22.3 | 33 |
| One Day at a Time | CBS | 1980–81 | 12 | 22.0 | 32 |
| Two of Us, The | CBS | 1980–81 | 13 | 21.8 | 33 |
| Little House on the Prairie | NBC | 1980–81 | 14 | 21.6 | 31 |

(Continued)

TABLE 1–1. (Continued)

| Program | Net | Season | Rank | Rtg. | Share |
|---|---|---|---|---|---|
| Archie Bunker's Place | CBS | 1980–81 | 15 | 21.4 | 32 |
| Greatest American Hero, The | ABC | 1980–81 | 16 | 21.1 | 32 |
| ABC NFL Monday Night Football | ABC | 1980–81 | 17 | 21.0 | 35 |
| Real People | NBC | 1980–81 | 18 | 20.9 | 32 |
| Magnum, P.I. | CBS | 1980–81 | 19 | 20.8 | 32 |
| Happy Days | ABC | 1980–81 | 20 | 20.8 | 32 |
| | | | | | |
| *HUT = 92,100,000* | | | | | |
| Cheers (19,617,300) | NBC | 1990–91 | 1 | 21.3 | 33 |
| 60 Minutes | CBS | 1990–91 | 2 | 20.6 | 35 |
| Roseanne | ABC | 1990–91 | 3 | 18.1 | 28 |
| Different World, A | NBC | 1990–91 | 4 | 17.5 | 28 |
| Cosby Show, The | NBC | 1990–91 | 5 | 17.1 | 27 |
| Murphy Brown | CBS | 1990–91 | 6 | 16.9 | 26 |
| Empty Nest | NBC | 1990–91 | 7 | 16.7 | 29 |
| America's Funniest Home Videos | ABC | 1990–91 | 8 | 16.7 | 26 |
| ABC NFL Monday Night Football | ABC | 1990–91 | 9 | 16.6 | 29 |
| Golden Girls, The | NBC | 1990–91 | 10 | 16.5 | 29 |
| Designing Women | CBS | 1990–91 | 11 | 16.5 | 25 |
| Murder, She Wrote | CBS | 1990–91 | 12 | 16.4 | 25 |
| America's Funniest People | ABC | 1990–91 | 13 | 16.3 | 25 |
| Full House | ABC | 1990–91 | 14 | 15.9 | 28 |
| Family Matters | ABC | 1990–91 | 15 | 15.8 | 27 |
| Unsolved Mysteries | NBC | 1990–91 | 16 | 15.7 | 25 |
| Matlock | NBC | 1990–91 | 17 | 15.5 | 24 |
| Coach | ABC | 1990–91 | 18 | 15.3 | 24 |
| Who's the Boss? | ABC | 1990–91 | 19 | 15.0 | 24 |
| CBS Sunday Night Movies | CBS | 1990–91 | 20 | 15.0 | 24 |

Abbreviation: HUT, homes using television.

scarcely any of the newcomers were in the same business as the networks. This brings us back to the question of interests and needs, and how they are met.

Each of us also has a need for information and entertainment that we think of as defining our individuality—the reverse of the shared interests mentioned earlier. We are antique car buffs, or dedicated fly fishermen, or bird watchers, or gardeners. We like ballet, or baroque music, or square dancing. These interests are less widespread, less commonly found

TABLE 1–2.  Population Forecasts

| Year | All Adults | % Dist. | 10–34 | % Dist. | 35–49 | % Dist. | 50+ | % Dist. |
|------|-----------|---------|-------|---------|-------|---------|-----|---------|
| 1992 | 189,450 | 100.0 | 88,205 | 36.0 | 55,320 | 29.2 | 65,925 | 34.8 |
| 1993 | 191,035 | 100.0 | 67,255 | 35.2 | 56,735 | 29.7 | 67,045 | 35.1 |
| 1994 | 192,585 | 100.0 | 66,305 | 34.4 | 58,305 | 30.3 | 67,975 | 35.3 |
| 1995 | 194,195 | 100.0 | 65,470 | 33.7 | 59,825 | 30.8 | 68,900 | 35.5 |
| 1996 | 195,780 | 100.0 | 64,540 | 33.0 | 61,495 | 31.4 | 69,745 | 35.6 |
| 1997 | 197,445 | 100.0 | 63,805 | 32.3 | 62,020 | 31.4 | 71,820 | 36.3 |
| 1998 | 199,100 | 100.0 | 63,165 | 31.7 | 62,740 | 31.5 | 73,195 | 36.3 |
| 1999 | 200,775 | 100.0 | 62,650 | 31.2 | 63,355 | 31.6 | 74,790 | 37.2 |
| 2000 | 202,380 | 100.0 | 62,120 | 30.7 | 63,955 | 31.6 | 76,305 | 37.7 |

*Source:* U.S. Bureau of the Census, Wilkofsky Gruen Associates

than the others. They are exclusive rather than inclusive (at their extreme, they are valued simply for their rarity).

These two types of interests—which we refer to as the process of aggregation and the process of disaggregation—or, more familiarly, the general and the specialized—are more compatible than competitive. They coexist in each of us, and therefore in society. Just as the networks exist in order to respond to the large-scale shared interests, the new technologies are directed at the smaller-scale interests. The actual result of this new order is mainly erosion at the networks' margins—most of it caused by competing with reruns of product they had originally developed. The networks' core function is little changed. So the changes that were anticipated as the decade began are not the ones that came about.

There are other reasons that there was such a rush to write the obituaries of the networks. One is the notion that a network is a monolithic power center—like the old Hollywood studios grown to gargantuan size. So a romantic giant killer mentality entered the equation (a mind-set that permeated the restrictive network legislation of the 1970s). In practice, a network is the centerpiece of a coalition. It manages a process. This gives it the executive role, and that is a potent one, but it does not own or control any of the other segments in the process. Its funding comes from scores of independent companies making their own advertising decisions. It buys the right to exhibit programs from another group of independent companies who retain ownership of the product. And it distributes those programs through agreements with stations owned by yet another group of independent companies. The system works for the usual reason: everybody involved benefits. More people watch these programs, so advertisers reach the largest possible audiences at the best rates of efficiency. Program suppliers get the highest prices for their product, and the affiliates get the most attractive product on the market.

The big lesson of this decade is the flexibility of the American system. New media arrive, but the old media do not disappear; they adjust. The adjustment is more complex than forecasters expect, and it never has all the anticipated results.

The network/affiliate system has survived in a world twenty times enlarged. The annual supply of television programs for prime time alone equals ten years of Hollywood film output or twenty-five years of Broadway. That cannot be achieved by a haphazard, hit-or-miss process. The keeper of this process through all these years has been the network/affiliate system. It is the spinal cord of the industry. Without its output, the other parts of the structure never could have developed. Community Antenna Television could not have grown into cable. There would be no CNN, and the VCR would be just another exotic piece of technology found in high-tech homes.

Behind all of this is the original technological marvel—the human mind. Whether they are put down by a quill dipped in ink or they appear on a PC screen, the lines have to be written, the scenes directed and acted. In the chapters that follow, we will look inside this creative part of the process.

# Chapter 2

# The Creative Product

Stacey Giles is seated at a word processor in a small office that could be anywhere but happens to be on the Universal lot in Los Angeles. She is one of four writers of a situation comedy called *Cloud Nine.*

*Cloud Nine* is in its third year on a network. In this sense it is a success. It is not, however, a hit. It has barely survived and is in serious trouble now, in February 1994. It is considered unlikely for renewal. This means that it might not make the critical fourth season, the season that would give it enough episodes for an afterlife as a rerun in the syndication market. On that depends any kind of serious profit for its owners.

Right now, Stacey is concerned only about the word processor screen in front of her. She is writing a scene for what could be the final episode of *Cloud Nine.* She is a skilled writer, widely read, clever, with a thorough knowledge of the medium and the form in which she is working. She has worked for Lear and Tinker and has written for *Cheers, The Cosby Show, Eight Is Enough,* and a lot of other shows that never got past the paper or pilot stage. *Cloud Nine* is not *Cheers* or *Cosby,* but it has made it through three seasons—barely—and just might make it to the fourth.

The scene Stacey is working on takes place at breakfast. She has written a lot of similar scenes. A meal is a situation. The situation part of situation comedy means what it says. The comedy arises from the manipulation of situations. There is first of all the main situation, the one all the characters share— the family, or workplace, or whatever it is, and their roles in it.

Then there are the immediate situations—the actual occasions that bring the characters together, togetherness being the necessary condition before anything funny can happen. There are two activities that account for most of the togetherness in a home. One is watching television. This is difficult to use for comic purposes because it does not naturally lead to dialogue. The other is meals, and the activity around meals. So characters in situation comedies eat a lot of meals, and they talk to each other before those meals and after those meals, and they have coffee breaks in between. They also eat when they visit their friends, are at work, or go out.

This particular breakfast scene includes the mother, her daughter, and the mother's live-in "friend." The friend, or fill-in father, is very sensitive about his non-daughter's activities, not out of any affection, but because he is terribly stuffy and feels her behavior reflects on him. This is ludicrous of course, and therefore it has comic possibilities. This scene will exploit this.

Stacey has in mind a sequence that involves the daughter telling the mother about last night's date, with the friend reading the newspaper and overhearing selected parts of the conversation. The comic moment she is trying to set up has the daughter answering the mother's question about who paid for the meal with the word *Dutch,* and then the question about what they ate with the word *Chinese.* The friend—only partly listening—mistakenly identifies the date, not the meal, as Chinese.

The timing and cutting to get this scene to work are very complex. Words and faces and reactions have to follow each other in a particular order, with split second precision. The friend's mistakenly connecting the word *date* with *Chinese* has to seem plausible. This will then allow one of the friend's set-piece, stuffed-shirt sputterings to be set off. (Sometimes called *stuffing,* these preset reaction bits are comic staples; entire motion picture careers were made on things like sneezes or slow burns.) But all this will happen only if Stacey can get the words *who* and *Chinese* closer together, while both remain part of a believable conversation. If she can work out this piece of business, she will have a little centerpiece around which she can build a solid two minutes of material. Not bad for a morning's work.

Out there are millions of people who would be astounded to learn how much effort two minutes of playing time takes. Only those who have had to do it know how hard it is to fill up that screen. Everyone else wonders why there aren't more hits. Where do they think it comes from? Stacey wonders. A weary network president once said to her, "What do they think we do—put something up there on the screen and say, 'That'll annoy them'?"Meanwhile, she is thinking that maybe this breakfast scene will work off a close-up of the friend with all the other lines overheard—then again, he would hear too much that way.

This is what the critics called "formula" programming: it is conventional, it is based on known ingredients, and it is familiar. Stacey knows that all comedy depends on the familiar. Man bites dog is funny only because we know that dogs usually bite men.

A scene about an Aztec breakfast would not be funny because nobody knows what an ordinary Aztec breakfast was like. A scene about an American breakfast can be funny precisely because there is a formula for it—not for the scene, per se, but for breakfast as a part of our collective experience. There are

formulas in life, and comedy depends on working disturbances
into them, disturbances just big enough to upset the normal
balance but not big enough to obscure the familiar pattern
underneath.

Stacey Giles is a link in a chain, but unlike the links in a
real chain, whose strength is their similarity, the links in this
chain are highly individualistic. The production chain is made
up of the singular characteristics of a variety of persons—their
talents, experiences, habits, hang-ups, energies, ambitions,
personalities, whatever. So each link is a risk. Down the line,
that chain connects with other chains. Television belongs to
the category known as the performing arts. The term *performing* presumes performing for some one—that is, an audience.
The final product is not the production itself, but the interac-
tion between the performed piece and the group for whom it is
being performed. In a theater, for instance, this might be
called the atmosphere that develops at the proscenium, the
space where the performers' actions and the audiences's reactions mix. In television, it is the space between the viewer
and the screen. In both cases, a judgment takes place at that
point, and in both cases, more often than not, it is a negative
one.

That is because it is a difficult thing to connect these two
chains successfully. A project can get under way with the highest of expectations, under the charge of a fine producer, using
award-winning performers, have a good script and a talented
director, and yet fail. It has been said that science is what is
repeatable. Art—whether it is the creation of grand opera or
situation comedy—certainly is not.

One classic attempt to rewrite that rule is the star system,
by which certain performers, in and of themselves, can make
inferior material acceptable. It has worked reasonably well over
the years, but for television there has been another puzzle: the
skills and sometimes even the forms that would seem to be
transferable between like media may not be.

For example, television can create new personalities, but it

This script and rehearsal conference of *Star Trek: Deep Space Nine* shows that television programs are a result of a collaboration of creative and talented people.
*Source:* Paramount Television

does not necessarily guarantee the continued success of stars from other media. Movie stars like Frank Sinatra, Gene Kelly, Jimmy Stewart, and Fred Astaire all had weekly television programs that were never huge hits. In contrast, Angela Lansbury, Lucille Ball, Candice Bergen, Carroll O'Connor, and Alan Alda are performers whose recognition on television far exceeded any previous recognition they had in the movies. Other performers, like Tom Selleck, Bill Cosby, William Shatner, and the many new faces from *Beverly Hills 90210,* became stars because of television.

This can be true for categories of fare as well. It is seldom recognized that network television made the National Football League, not vice versa. The league had been in existence for many decades prior to television. It is only with network exposure that the NFL has grown to such gigantic proportions in today's sport world. On the other hand, hockey and soccer have not been able to enjoy similar success, probably because they are both difficult to watch and to broadcast. With little viewer interest in them, there is little advertiser interest, and little interest in providing the kind of exposure given to professional football. But that brings us to the function of another part of another chain in the system—schedule decisions.

In another part of Los Angeles, Pat French, thirty-eight, a network scheduler, is sitting in his office staring at a board showing the prime-time schedules of the three networks. It looks like an enormous calendar on which the days always appear three times. This board displays the elements of the chess game Pat is paid to play. He must move shows just the way chess players move pieces, deciding on what day and at what time to put what show. Each move has the same effect that it has on a chessboard: by moving one piece, the value of every other piece is changed. In this case, however, there are three pieces in every square, each trying to occupy the same space at the same time. Anything one loses, another gains. And, unlike real chess, the power of each piece is only partly—if at all—predictable.

Pat has been playing schedule chess for five years. To do so, he needs to assign a value to his pieces and to his competitors' pieces. He also needs to decide where the pieces are likely to be. For this, he needs good sources around town and in New York, in the production community and in the advertising community.

Five years ago he had to worry about only the other two networks. Everything he scheduled was against them. Now he has six, seven, or eight competitors to worry about. A big movie or a big sports event on pay cable can hurt him.

His job is to put in place the pieces that make up one thousand hours a year of prime time on his network. Most homes now get twenty channels. That adds up to twenty thousand hours of prime time a year. That is more than all the movies that have been made in Pat's lifetime. More than all the Broadway plays that have been produced in this century.

Pat French doesn't know Stacey Giles, but he knows *Cloud Nine* only too well. He knows its rating on every date this season and on every date of the two previous seasons: how it did against every show opposite it and every show it played after and what it did for every show that followed it. And he has the same information on all of its competitors, too. He is inclined to think that *Cloud Nine* will not be back next season, but, since this isn't a sure thing, he has prepared estimates for it on tentative schedules on three different nights against four possible competitive schedules.

Pat could write the biography of every show that has appeared on any network in the past eight years. While there are always exceptions—shows brought in by stars, shows "owed" to a producer or an agent—a likely progression would begin in some production organization with a history in the medium. There, a few senior people work over a number of concepts in highly informal—but not uninformed—discussions. Each of them knows a good deal about what the public is likely to accept and what it is not, and about what it is possible to put on the screen and what it is not. This means that there is an automatic, prediscussion process of elimination derived from extensive personal experience before the first words are even uttered. Eventually they come to a point where one idea meets the fundamental requirements, has some distinctive qualities, and is ready to be described. It is, say, a comedy set in a real estate office. They see in this setting a number of attractive structural features: familiarity—since everyone at some point deals with real estate people, most of the audience can easily identify with them; informality—it is the nature of these places that they are loosely structured and entirely people-centered; variety—since it is an ubiquitous profession that touches everyone, mobility—since it reaches out everywhere into the community: intensity—since these are often the most serious transactions people ever undertake. They know these features are valued by actors, writers, and directors as well as by audiences because they allow lots of story and character possibilities. Next, they work up a concept, describing the setting and the proposed principal players and outlining a number of story ideas. They bring their concept to a network program-development person, who asks for changes and clarification but agrees to consider it. The revised concept is analyzed, dissected, gone over at length at the network, and revised again and ordered into script. A budget for this stage is now provided by the network, and the script again undergoes intensive examination and is rewritten several more times. Finally a decision is made to produce a pilot—also funded by the network. Now a production team and a cast must be assembled, initiating a phase of business procedures that again alter aspects of the concept (who is available, for example, impinges on what roles are set and how the characters will be interpreted). The pilot is then screened and tested. If the indications are good enough, a production order is given, perhaps for only six or seven episodes. The show is then included in a package of possible entries for the next season, which in turn are eventually measured against the needs of the schedule as they are defined at the end of the present season (for example, how many replacements are needed and of these, how many comedies, dramas, movies, etc., how many hour or half-hour forms are needed; what time periods are most vulnerable/desirable; what the likely competition is). Eventually, the show is given a specific time period and the final jury, the viewers, take over.

Pat French is in touch with this entire process, but his major role is at the end, after the product exists. He is not a writer or producer, but he knows how many two-minute breakfast scenes he needs to get near a thousand usable hours a year.

The most familiar aspect of what is called the Dictatorship

of Numbers is at work here. Stacey Giles and Pat French are hoping to reach every viewer they can. This is the lust for the mass audiences that critics say inevitably leads toward mediocrity—the hackneyed, the trite, the unimaginative. There are certainly no illusions that *Cloud Nine* is likely to provoke deep thoughts or provide startling insights. The hope is that it will provide some diversion—more, at any rate, than anything else on at the time.

The implication behind the Dictatorship of Numbers is that it leads to an automatic process, a safe haven, free of the risks of "real" creativity. But all shows—even *Cloud Nine*—fall victim to a much more subtle aspect of the Dictatorship of Numbers—perhaps the oldest dictatorship of all. This is the Rule of Scarcity, which says there will never be enough talent. Failure is the rule in every creative enterprise dependent on popular support—books, plays, songs, movies. Failure persists across even the most successful careers in each of these fields. Individuals, partners, and production teams who have succeeded at one time fail at another, often with what seem to be the very same ingredients. Whether Stacey Giles is going to provoke deep thoughts or provide startling insights is not the problem; the problem is that there are not enough of her to go around even when far more modest goals are sought.

Pat French's network will review two thousand program ideas a year. About 250 of these will be judged good enough to go on into the script form. About thirty to forty of the scripts will move along into pilot production. About ten pilots will make it into series form. Perhaps two or three series will survive into a second season or longer. The process costs $50 to $60 million a year. In other businesses it is known as Research and Development. In television it is called failure, or futility, or a wasteland.

Some form of a Dictatorship of Numbers is at work in every business. Whatever the enterprise, there is a product, there must be a means of getting it to the customers, and someone must be willing to pay for it. This interrelated cycle—production, distribution, and funding—is its own Dictatorship of Numbers. If the costs of distribution and production outweigh the income from sales, there is no business. In television, sales and the size of the audience are directly related, and that is the nexus of the Dictatorship of Numbers.

It is not that there is anything sinister in this connection per se; the term is one of opprobrium for those who feel that television ought to have a higher purpose than reaching large numbers of people. But their case does not rest there, for it depends in the end on the belief that those large numbers of people—and the greater society—would be better served by some more compelling material even if they do not wish to watch it.

Regardless of those who believe networks should provide very special kinds of programs that may attract only a limited audience, networks have been and must remain generalists. To survive, they must reach out to the broadest possible range of interests and needs among the broadest possible segments of viewers. Those interests and needs change, partly as the society changes, and partly as the media environment changes. A good example of change induced by the competitive environment is Saturday morning, a time period that was for more than a generation devoted almost exclusively to children's programming.

In the 1980s several developments occurred in this area. First, the FCC enacted new regulations restricting certain commercial practices. Consequently, the networks were prevented from permitting commercial-program tie-ins—that is, sponsorship where the product being sold was also an integral part of the program in which the commercial for it appeared. While the networks in general had already imposed limitations on this practice, the result was that the tie-in category of advertising, along with its programming, immediately became a growth market for the independents. In addition, whole new channels devoted entirely to children's programming had appeared, such as The Disney Channel and Nickelodeon. More channels meant more competition for both audiences and advertisers in a programming genre where the afterlife of the product was phenomenal. There seemed to be almost no limit to the number of times a child would watch the same episode. So evident was this that the networks eventually found they could limit themselves to only thirteen new cartoon episodes per year— which meant four repeats—without damaging audience levels. Moreover, the audience renewed itself every three or four years. This meant that the big advantage the networks had enjoyed by offering more new product was relatively less effective here than elsewhere. Finally, some of the networks' affiliates began preempting the Saturday morning lineup, weakening the other paramount network advantage, total distribution. In these circumstances, NBC has already abandoned the children's genre on Saturday morning, and the other networks are looking hard at the benefits of retaining the status quo. In the midst of this indecision, the Fox Network has managed to take advantage of the NBC decision and now reaches more children on Saturday morning than any of the "Big 3."

The quest for more effective use of time periods has been a major issue since the beginning of networking as a business. In 1978, one time period that came under examination was Sunday morning. For years CBS, in cooperation with the Council of Churches, had broadcast two programs, *Lamp unto My Feet* and *Look up and Live*. Despite the fact that these programs had been on for so long, very few viewers watched them. The reason was not lack of quality but lack of distribution: only some twenty-two out of more than two hundred affiliates cleared the programs. And the reason behind that was lack of funding. These were sustaining, or noncommercial, programs. In fact, this situation is a graphic example of the need for a proportionate relationship among the distribution-production-funding aspects of the business. A severe breakdown in any one of the three is eventually fatal. That simple fact helped to persuade the Council of Churches that the communities around the country would be better served if the network provided a news broadcast on Sunday in addition to other special programs dealing with religious issues.

The genesis of that program idea took place during a European Broadcasters' Conference in Greece, which Gene was attending with Bill Leonard, who was then in charge of CBS's Washington office. It was there that Gene asked Bill to become the president of CBS news. Bill brought to the job an extraordinary combination of reportorial, production, and executive experience. He had been a reporter and producer at both the radio and television flagship stations of the network in New York. He had both produced and reported documentaries for the network. He had headed the network's election and documentary production units and the corporation's Washington office. He was also a world-class ham radio operator. With his knowledge and experience in all aspects of news, he was prepared to be an extremely able president. It was at that meeting that Bill and Gene discussed the concept that eventually became *Sunday Morning* with Charles Kuralt as the original anchorman. After fifteen years, he was followed by Charles Osgood.

That program not only received great critical acclaim, but, by serving a wider interest, it reached substantially more viewers than anything else on Sunday morning. In so doing, it also improved the profits of the network. Because of the success of CBS in this time period, ABC and NBC eventually introduced new Sunday morning programming as well.

A wider audience and greater profits are, of course, the goals behind every programming decision, even if they are not always reachable. The same goals drive decisions in prime time, too. This reality led many people to view a decision CBS made as based on politics and not on performance when it canceled *Lou Grant*.

*Lou Grant* was a program in which quality ingredients did have the desired result. It brought pride to all those associated with it, and it attracted substantial audiences. Its star, Ed Asner, remains one of Hollywood's finest performers, a gifted man who has the talent to play a broad range of roles, from light comedy to serious drama, with equal skill. He brought enormous conviction to the central role of the city editor of a large newspaper. He was the means of entry into the stories, which revolved around issues and situations, many of them controversial, that were current in society. Yet it was Asner's very success that was to become the source of the problems associated with the program.

There is a factor known as program fatigue, a wearing down of effectiveness that tends to set in after a certain number of years. Sometimes introducing new cast members or new faces on the production team can offset it. The trick lies in judging exactly when it has become critical, when a program has gone past a point of no return. By 1982, *Lou Grant* had been on the schedule for three years—a long span by television standards—and was beginning to show signs of fatique. While it still had a loyal core following, the less frequent viewers were abandoning it, and the margin of success depended on their presence. Of course, a cancellation decision implies a replacement decision. The question was whether there was a replacement that would have both the quality and durability that *Lou Grant* had. Unfortunately, coincidental with the decision-making process regarding *Lou Grant,* Ed Asner made some controversial political remarks as a private citizen. The backlash created a minor story in the press. CBS was accused of bending to pressure in deciding on the cancellation. That this was not the case is demonstrated by the fact that the replacement program was *Cagney and Lacey,* also a serious drama that touched on social issues, and also featuring outstanding performing talent, in this case two actresses cast as New York City police officers—leadership roles usually associated with men.

The program stayed on the air for seven years, and some of the show's performers won numerous awards.

Both *Sunday Morning* and *Cagney and Lacey* demonstrate how improving the service in a time period leads to improved revenues. The cynical phrase in the industry is that the networks are in business "to sell eyeballs to advertisers." What the phrase overlooks is that those eyeballs, the viewers, have to be there to begin with. A network must make its decisions based on viewers' interests before anything else. Advertising values are derived from the viewers' interests, not the other way around.

To add some perspective to the *Lou Grant* story, it should be noted that it is rare for any network entertainment program to last more than four years. The creative skills required to produce a weekly program that endures are in very short supply. This is because television reverses the traditional relationship between audience and content. In both the legitimate theater and the movies, the product stays the same, and the audience changes. In television, just the opposite occurs. The audience is always there, so the product must change. It is hard to find materials that are able to stand up under the repeated exposure television demands, where familiarity and freshness have to be combined. To last four years is outstanding; to last eight is exceptional; to last more than ten is phenomenal. In the history of television only fifty-six programs have ever done so.

## Creativity and the Nature of the System

The collective resources of the network-affiliate combination are extraordinary: more than twenty thousand employees, most of them at more than two hundred stations, and almost $7 billion, half of it spent by the stations, is required to operate one network. There is no comparable system anywhere in the world. Nor is there any competitor in America able to deploy these resources behind a single channel of communication.

Still, is it fair to ask here, why is size so critical? Isn't it, after all, the solitary genius who stands behind the creative process? There are two answers to the size question. First, is that actual production in television (like motion pictures) is a collaborative process that involves a large amount of highly sophisticated labor and equipment. Wherever the idea might have originated, getting it onto the screen is very expensive. So there is a heavy cost factor built in right away. And second, there is a hidden multiple to be applied to this. In television, as in all creative endeavors, the rule is failure. There will be at least four or five flops for every hit. And the flops cost just as much to make as the hits. This is why everyone in the business eventually learns that in order to find the hits, you have to fund the failures.

Even then there are hazards. Film studios have to hope that the profits from the big hit blockbusters will cover the costs of the failures or the specialized, limited-audience productions that are on their schedules. There is no guarantee that this will work out—a recent example being the case of Orion Pictures, which had serious financial problems in the same year in which it produced some of the biggest hits in the industry.

While there are no Newtonian calculations that will reliably predict what will rise and what will fall, the following maxims, regarding the creative process and its practitioners are widely accepted as having the stature of laws:

Law Number One: When something is made from nothing, most often it will be a failure (anything times zero still equals zero).

Law Number Two: Even as a failure, the cost of production will be more than originally estimated. (This is anti–lunar gravity law: Production budgets get heavier after launching.)

To these laws can be added a psychological given: after the failure, the creator will discover that somebody or something else was responsible for whatever went wrong. This is an irritant; but it is more than that. It can obscure the search for the real reasons and thereby affect future decisions in the same area. It is very important that failure be understood.

So there is a dismaying amount of negative arithmetic at work: if it costs $1.2 million to produce every original hour of a successful network drama, it has also cost that much to produce the three or four other program ideas that never go on the air. If the successful version runs long enough, it will overcome this drag on its profitability, but the fact remains that it is on only because it emerged from the pack in the first place. The pack—all $4 or $5 million of it—had to be there for it to be found.

This situation is not unique to motion pictures or television. Procter & Gamble, Bristol Myers, Colgate, Lever Brothers, Johnson & Johnson, Ford, General Motors, IBM—in fact, all companies operating in a highly competitive market economy—must fund costly Research and Development programs if they hope to remain successful.

Yet, in spite of this universal truth, there is a strong tendency to think otherwise when it comes to the creative product. Here, optimism prevails. Perhaps it begins with the word *Creative* itself, which is usually taken to signify something that stands apart from concepts like planning or process or formulae for historic rates of failure. It is not only tempting to ignore these pedestrian factors; it can even seem noble to do so.

Perhaps it is also because creativity originates in a purely cerebral environment, in the deep recesses of the individual psyche. An air of mystery surrounds it. It is not traceable on a blueprint; its speed and direction cannot be calculated; its weight and size are undetermined. It is a kind of magic, and it might strike anywhere.

For a risk taker, the final appeal to create something new might be that all of these aspects and even the ultimate materials themselves—merely words and actions—are virtually cost free. The gamble is simply that when these words and actions are arranged in this or that particular sequence, they will capture the interest of the audience. One does not have to build a factory, hire workers, purchase raw materials, manufacture the product, package it, and then ship it to market to find out if the gamble paid off.

Whatever the reasons, the lure is fabled. And it is not confined to purely "creative" product, as it would usually be defined. There is a corresponding temptation to believe that because the means of delivering information exists, there is some automatic value in delivering it, regardless of the circumstances of the market for which it is intended.

## The Program-Supply Problem

As television advanced from five channels to ten, then twenty, then thirty, and now fifty and moving toward one hundred, as VCRs, cable, and satellites came into play, as broadcasters watched their positions erode, the questions became which audiences to reach for and where, when, and how.

It was complicated in the old three-network world, which represented thirty-six hundred hours in prime time alone every year. The rest of the network time periods added another fifteen thousand hours. That did not count local time—time filled individually by the stations—roughly another three thousand hours. Where was some fifty thousand hours of sight, sound, and motion to come from? There were fewer than one thousand hours of motion pictures made in a year. Broadway turned out fewer than two hundred hours a year. It was a staggering proposition to begin with, and then cable introduced a means of expanding distribution overnight. A twenty-channel system meant twenty-four thousand hours of prime time. If it was on the air fifteen hours a day, it was going to need over one hundred thousand hours of material annually (more hours of prime time than CBS has broadcast in its entire history!).

A major part of the solution for this critical question is

found once again in old motion pictures and reused television series. For example, in one single week, August 16–22, 1992, according to the television guide in the Sunday *New York Times*, there were 376 movies scheduled. This represents about 750 hours of programming provided by motion pictures for that week. Most of the movies were more than fifteen years old. One hundred and twenty of them were more than thirty years old. While this is only one week, it would be interesting to find out how many times these movies were repeated during the course of the full year. One can assume that they would be substantially repeated within the year and many, many times over the decade. The cost requirement of producing new programs to fill the time requirements would be astronomical! Once again, the Dictatorship of Numbers is at work. New programs are expensive. Old movies are not, but since circulation is low, so is income (Table 2–1).

An explosion in the means of distribution had occurred. In earlier times, a network had to produce its way into competition. ABC did not become fully competitive until the mid '70s, twenty years after its founding, when it could place its own lineups opposite those of CBS and NBC in all the major dayparts. Cable, on the other hand, began life as a reception improver, not a maker of product. It still relies on the product

TABLE 2–1. Week of August 16–22, 1992—Number of Motion Pictures per Decade

| | |
|------|-----|
| 1920 | 2 |
| 1930 | 31 |
| 1940 | 59 |
| 1950 | 36 |
| 1960 | 39 |
| 1970 | 42 |
| 1980 | 85 |
| 1990 | 82 |
| Total | 376 |

of the over-the-air systems, which continues to be its biggest attractions.

As channels multiplied without compensating increases in production capacity, television was becoming its own supply-side economy without the supply. The Dictatorship of Numbers had taken on a new meaning.

In 1980, an FCC chairman told broadcasters, "I am not your shepherd, and you are not my flock." Then, in 1991, the Commission found it necessary to issue a study that suggested that broadcasters were an endangered species with an uncertain future. What does that mean? The full input of each of the network-affiliate partnerships represents an annual expenditure of about $7 billion a year. The networks and their affiliates together annually spend $21 billion. Their investment accounts for the overwhelming bulk of the programming that drives the entire system.

We once had networks without cable. Any number of commentators have suggested that the future might bring the reverse, that the fabled "dinosaurs" are on an irreversible path to extinction. The hard facts of the case—that is, the realities of the production-distribution-funding cycle—do not support any such conclusion.

More on the specifics of the way the business operates is covered in the next chapter. How advertising rates are determined and other sources of funding are discussed. Mention is also made of the importance of stations affiliated with the networks, and how they affect the distribution system that continues to be one of network television's greatest assets. Essentially, the network television business is as complex as a Rubik's Cube.

# Chapter *3*

# Where the Money Comes From

He was waiting for the 7:02, just as he had done mornings for the twenty-nine years he had lived in Connecticut. The platform was crowded with commuters like himself, some of them neighbors, but on this particular morning he felt lonely and separate from the crowd. Peter Francis was the senior vice president for network sales at a major broadcasting company. It was hard to believe that thirty-two years had gone by since he had joined the company as a young salesman fresh out of graduate school. He had accomplished a lot during those years—advancement, financial reward—but lately something was eating away at his sense of security.

How complicated the business had become since those days when he first joined the network. Sales back then followed a standard procedure. Advertisers such as General Foods would buy into programs for fifty-two weeks, and that was that until next year. Or, even better, sometimes the clients brought their own programs to the network, and all the salesperson had to do was sell them a time period. Once that was done, it was a service job—lunches and entertainment and lots of golf with clients who were usually intelligent and stimulating people.

All that had changed now. Sales were far more complicated, much faster, and, in an expanded and still rapidly changing media environment, hectic and confusing. Some people, even industry leaders, were jumping to conclusions about which he had serious reservations. He sometimes thought he was the only person who felt this way, a lonely holdout in the crowd.

Peter worried that some attitudes within the network itself were a threat to its own economic survival. One recent decision endorsed accepting commercials that invited viewers to subscribe to cable TV and pay TV. Would General Motors urge its customers to buy a Chrysler or a Honda? Would CBS sell advertising time to NBC? There were other areas of concern about which Peter felt strongly, areas that he believed needed to be reexamined and perhaps rethought. Books about television were published every few months, but most of them dealt with the gossip and personalities of the industry, not with the substance, the reality that confronted Peter day by day. At the heart of this reality lay a complex business equation that was almost never referred to in books and articles. If you wanted to understand television in America, where it had come from and where it was going, you had to understand that equation. In Peter's mind, the equation was like a popular game from the 1980s—solving the puzzle of Rubik's Cube. Rubik's Cube is a large cube composed of layers of smaller cubes. Each layer can be rotated separately. The goal is to get the layers to line up so that each side of the entire cube is the same color. The problem is that when one layer is rotated to match a color on one side the colors on all the other sides change.

Peter's side of the cube was sales, but he'd had to learn that a sales decision, which is basically a funding decision, is also a programming decision and a distribution decision. To move his side of the cube was to affect all the other sides. Therefore, a program decision is also a sales decision and a distribution decision. To ignore this equation seemed to him a fatal flaw in what was currently happening in the television industry. And so he felt isolated and estranged as he waited on the train platform for the 7:02.

While Peter Francis is a fictitious character, his concerns are not. In the era of new technologies' rapid growth, distribution is the side of the cube that has received all the attention. Rarely are the production or funding implications considered. Yet it is the strength of each component and the balance among them that determine success. For example, while there have been frequent anncouncements of a new technology offering up to five hundred channels, reference is seldom made to costs, programming, sales, or even the needs these channels would fill (in one case the only program idea mentioned was reruns of *60 Minutes*). Another idea concerned a means of transmitting forty-nine new channels directly to a home antenna. It, too, ignored the question of costs and programming, as well as the fact that transmitting directly to the home is hardly new. Radio and television stations have been doing that for sixty years. The issue isn't getting a signal there, but providing content that will hold an audience. In the network scheme of things, that content comes from both the resources of the affiliated stations, with their local programming, and the network, with its nationwide programming. With this combination, each network provides eight thousand hours of programming a year, the equivalent of about ten years' worth of Hollywood feature films. When new services are announced, the production dimension of the cube is conveniently ignored because the task of matching this is far beyond the resources of any new entry, even though these services are invariably trumpeted as threats to the networks.

Whatever the means of delivery, the Rubik's Cube relationships are the underpinnings of the business. How do they apply in the new exploding television universe? In this chapter we address the various components of the network-business equation.

### Creation, Production, and Observations about Scheduling and Sales

It used to be axiomatic that the network with the highest ratings would also be the most profitable. But this did not happen in the network 1991–92 season. And it did not happen in 1992–93.

The CBS Television Network ranked number one in ratings. However, in the network's race for ratings, it paid too much for programming that could not be sold at prices high enough to cover operating costs. In 1991–92, despite eliminating more than four hundred jobs, reducing network compensation, and cutting back on program expenditures, the CBS Network had a loss of over $200 million. On the other hand, the ABC Television Network finished third and made a profit. NBC finished second with a modest profit, and the fledgling Fox Network finished fourth with a profit, making its affiliated stations happy with improved ratings and higher revenues.

These results indicate that a number of the assumptions behind network procedures that originated in the early 1960s need to be reevaluated in the 1990s. In today's competitive environment these include the use of reruns, the length of the television season, and the sweeps, those periods when the A. C. Nielsen Company periodically measures the viewing audiences of television stations around the country on a market-by-market basis. The three most important sweeps are in May, November, and February. The prices stations charge for local advertisements are based on these ratings. As a result, stations and the networks make an extraordinary effort to schedule the best and often the most provocative broadcasts during these three months. The practice is expensive and often deceptive, since it can result in ratings that are not representative of a station's normal audience during the rest of the year. If the practice were eliminated, networks and stations could more effectively schedule their stronger programs throughout the year, optimize circulation, and maximize revenue. As it is, strong programs are often scheduled against other strong programs, with the result that the audience loses an opportunity to enjoy more than one popular show. If the viewer is able to tape one of the programs, it is viewed at a later time, only to take audience away from some other show. Programs are assets. Optimum realization of those assets could be made possible by eliminating sweeps.

Networks have made periodic attempts either to lengthen the sweeps to twelve weeks or to eliminate them, only to be challenged by the affiliates who feel any change would cost them more for programming. The stations need to be persuaded that in view of the large number of new competitors, in the long term it is in the mutual best interests of both the stations and the networks to address the sweeps issue.

Similarly, if contemporary electronic distribution systems are capable of delivering thirty-five or more programs into the home at any given time, it seems wasteful to spend unprofitable dollars in a thirty-week race to finish first in what is only a three-player race. The network season that historically begins in September and ends in April is a throwback to the era when being number one in ratings also meant being number one in profits. This artificial arrangement was established in the economic self-interest of the networks, not in response to the needs of the audience. It worked when three entrants played on the same field with the same ground rules. It is outmoded in a thirty-five-channel world where rules may differ by player.

It is worth looking into broadcast-season history in order to better understand the origins of the race. The original broadcast season was thirty-nine weeks, that is, fall, winter, and spring. Then there was a summer hiatus. The program for the remaining thirteen weeks was filled by a different original series. For example, *The Jack Benny Program* was broadcast for thirty-nine weeks, and while Benny took a thirteen-week hiatus, viewers could watch *The Herb Shriner Show*. On NBC one year, *The Dean Martin Show* was replaced during the summer months by *Dean Martin Presents the Golddiggers*, a variety program featuring Frank Sinatra, Jr., and Joey Heatherton. Thus, the stars received time off for other activities, and the network was able to broadcast other new programs.

This situation began to change in the early 1960s, when an alert network executive with a sharp pencil and an appreciation for the bottom line suggested that if the network scheduled reruns of the best of regular-season shows, the network would save a substantial amount of money. Thus, original summer replacement programs gave way to reruns of series episodes. Philosophically, what had actually occurred was that the financial needs of the network took precedence over the desires of the audience. Fortunately for the networks, the only other channels viewers could turn to in most cities were the other networks. With the exception of independent stations in large cities, it was basically a zero-sum game for the audience. Eventually, the thirty-nine-week commitment became twenty-six and then twenty-two.

The decision to decrease the number of original weeks was prompted by financial concerns. As cable began to evolve during the 1980s, more program choices became available. Also, the introduction of the videocassette recorder provided the home viewer with an almost unlimited supply of programs, including instant reruns. The increase in independent television stations and the introduction of the Fox Television Network also created more viewing choices. A three-network race on the old thirty-nine week track in the midst of all this competition would be foolish. Furthermore, as a result of the increased competition, the networks are now faced with the difficult task of increasing the number of original hours of programming while minimizing the financial impact.

And the financial impact can be severe. In 1993, the licensing fee paid by a network to a supplier for a one-hour program was about $1 million. The actual cost to produce that program might be $200,000 more than the fee. In the case of half-hour programs, the licensing fee might be about $425,000, while the actual cost of production might be closer to $600,000. The deficit is absorbed by the producer, who hopes that sufficient ratings success will enable enough episodes to be produced for future foreign and domestic syndication to recover the shortfall. This high cost for programs also works against a major rapid return to more original broadcasts.

In the same way that network schedules evolved into fewer weeks of original programs, evolution is the key to building more original programs back into the yearly schedules. The networks cannot afford the huge financial costs associated with original programs by reversing the process quickly. Advertisers will pay for circulation, but only after research shows what programs will deliver in audience reach. Furthermore, the amount of money available for television advertising is finite, and it is usually determined on an annual basis. Even if a network could demonstrate that a summer schedule of completely new programs was drawing large numbers of viewers, advertising dollars would flow more slowly after those viewers because of the way clients' budgeting processes work. It would be a slow and difficult process. In the end, the networks would be well advised to discard the old thirty-nine-week standard and concentrate on maximizing circulation over the full year.

It cannot be restated often enough that it is programming that attracts viewers. While some program decisions have been made, and in all likelihood will continue to be made, primarily for financial reasons, this philosophy can lead to problems. In 1987, CBS scheduled four new series to replace a weekly movie, basically because the four shows were less expensive than the movie. It was highly probable, based on the historical performance of new programs, that a movie would attract more viewers than the group of new series. As predicted, the new programs failed, and CBS finished in third place for the season. If there had been no race, this would have been a non-event. As it was, the negative publicity cost the network future profits because the story about finishing last contributed to lower sales. Creative investments may be risky, but cost-driven decisions often turn out to be even more risky.

Another important reason for networks to improve the summer schedule relates to local-station options. Because of the number of new syndicated programs that are available, affiliated stations that are dissatisfied with the performance of certain network programs are often willing to replace a network rerun with a syndicated program. This is especially likely if the network has cut station compensation. Every station that does not carry a network origination weakens the lineup for the network. Fewer stations means smaller audiences, and smaller audiences mean smaller revenues. At some point in this chain, the program, and possibly even a network, is no longer viable.

The cost for programs is always a serious consideration, yet, as one network executive put it, "the costs don't matter if the jokes are funny!" That statement sounds more frivolous than it is. The high cost of a successful show can be offset not only by high advertising rates, but by its influence in other areas, such as the audience support it provides for the shows around it in the lineup, or relationships with some of the most sought-after talents in the creative community. There is a history of successful spin-offs of hit shows, not only in the direct sense of transferring established characters to new shows, such as creating *Lou Grant* and *Rhoda* out of *The Mary Tyler Moore Show,* but also in the transfer of proven creative talent to new shows. Finally, once established, hits are predictable, a very important factor in a business where the advertising investments have to be made before exposure.

It is also obvious that expensive programs can fail—in fact, more often than not, they do. But for a network there is risk in approaching the equation from the cost end if the strategy is to accept lower ratings in exchange for lower costs. For example, there has been a recent trend to put news division–produced programs into their prime-time schedules because they bring with them three kinds of potential cost savings. First, they cost only about half what an entertainment program would cost. Second, the networks own them and thus automatically have rerun rights and do not have to negotiate with an outside source for renewal. And third, by using an existing production resource, they help to amortize the overall cost of the news operation. All these are attractive features, but there is also a downside. Each substitution of a low-cost news or reality show for an entertainment program decreases the chance of developing a big hit. It also lowers the overall average rating of the network. This approach is analogous to a professional baseball team refusing to pay high salaries for big stars. A team may be put on the field, but it will not win many pennants. In the end, the total gross rating points a network generates—that is, the combined ratings of all of its shows—are its source of revenue. It is never to the network's advantage to decrease this figure intentionally.

Predictability, one of the prime assets of established hits, is also a paramount factor in another area where critical cost decisions are made—namely, sports, which has an added dimension that is more difficult to gauge—emotional attachment. In a real sense, major sports attractions are already established hits: they are part of the culture, with their own identity and their own following. These are very appealing charcteristics for broadcasters, but that does not mean there is no risk. The future can be mortgaged because of long-term expensive sports commitments. Or they can be pots of gold. Here are examples illustrating the difficulties inherent in making such judgments.

Just after Gene became president of the Broadcast Group, the National Football League contract was expiring, and nego-

Television has popularized professional sports with the financial support of advertisers. (Photo by Tim Defrisco)
*Source:* National Basketball Association

tiations were about to begin on a new four-year pact. The previous contract had required CBS to pay $22 million per year. Gene was told that a new four-year deal would cost $44 million per season, a breath-stopping change. No matter how loyal the fans were, certainly the audience could not double from one year to the next. The package was analyzed carefully for economic impact, but there was also a powerful non-numerical element at play. Gene knew that the executive who rejected the NFL proposal would probably have to tell the affiliates there would be no Sunday afternoon football on their stations. This was a cherished tradition in an absolutely crucial relationship whose value went beyond ordinary calculations. CBS signed up. The bonus was that by the end of the four-year contract, a substantial profit was made. As it turned out, advertisers shared the affiliates' evaluation of the product and absorbed the increase.

Then, in December of 1993, the unthinkable happened. The fledgling Fox Network outbid CBS for the rights to the National Football Conference Division games of the NFL. CBS executives were "shell-shocked," according to a report in the *New York Times*. In a bidding contest for the rights, Fox promised to pay over $100 million more than CBS offered for TV coverage, a total estimated to be close to $1.6 billion over four years, an average annual payment of almost $400 million. And, for the first time in almost forty years, CBS would not be carrying the NFC games. The repercussions of that event will be felt throughout the network and its affiliates for many years to come! Losing the NFC games to Fox might be considered the modern equivalent of NBC losing Jack Benny to CBS in the mid-1940s. Broadcast historians recognize that that acquisition led to CBS's gaining equal stature with NBC as a major network.

This was followed in May 1994 by an even bigger surprise. Fox shocked the broadcast world by obtaining twelve major new affiliates, eight of them from CBS. This is the largest single movement of affiliates in the industry's history. As we have said elsewhere, despite all the claims made for the various 'new technologies', none of them has a distribution system to equal that of the networks—the access to virtually every home in the nation provided by affiliates. Moreover, affiliates are a program source and an established local presence in their own right. They are traffic providers as well as traffic directors. The distinctive aspect of a network is its ability to integrate local and national services into a continuous, balanced flow, to maintain the trilogy that lies at the heart of the business, the production–distribution–funding cycle. Affiliates are obviously an indispensable component of this process. Rupert Murdoch, Chairman and Chief Executive of Fox, as a latecomer, has had to ratchet Fox up, building programming, affiliates, and funding a notch at a time. In this instance, he is simultaneously upgrading his own distribution capacity and damaging that of a major competitor in a single move. His investment is a stunning reaffirmation of confidence in the original, over-the-air technology.

In 1989, CBS found itself in the opposite position, namely, offering more than the competition and substantially overpaying, in this case, for baseball. It should be added that baseball carries with it a greater risk than football. Unlike football, the big baseball attractions do not offer a guaranteed inventory because the exact number of games to be played cannot be forecast. The combination of playoffs and world series can be as few as ten or as many as seventeen games, and virtually all of the profit is in the larger number. As a result, even in 1992, when the prime-time schedule for CBS made that network number one in the ratings, the network did not make a profit. This was the first time in history when the number one network lost money.

A long rating history shows that baseball in general is not as attractive as football to television audiences. The scarcity of major professional games is the reason football does so well. So long as the National Football League limits exposure and prices the rights fees at a level that allows broadcasters to carry

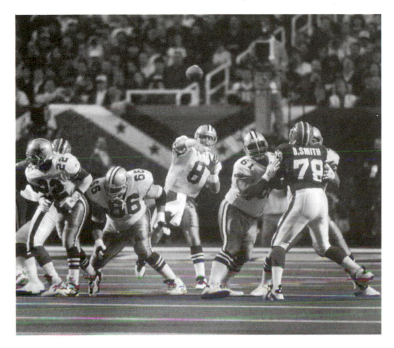

The 1994 Super Bowl was viewed by more than 134,800,000 people and is claimed to be the largest domestic audience in television history. (Photograph by Mark Sherengo)
*Source:* National Football League

the games profitably, football will continue to be on free television. If, in the drive for more and greater revenues, the NFL owners were to move from free TV to pay TV, they would be planting the seeds for large legal and financial problems. It should be noted that it was network television that made professional football the institution it has become, not the other way around.

## Funding, the Financial Support of the Product

The revenues needed to cover the cost of television programs can be derived in three ways—advertiser support, subscriptions, and pay.

One of the largest advertisers on television is the Coca Cola Company, which spends more than one hundred and fifty million dollars annually. This photo features football's Mean Joe Greene in one of the company's most highly acclaimed and most memorable commercials.
*Source:* Coca Cola Co.

Pay television is an extension of a service originally known as Community Antenna Television (CATV), which, as its name implies, was a shared connection to a bigger antenna, to offer viewers a clearer picture of the existing channels. People were willing to pay for that service.

It was only later that cable was used to transmit additional channels. Here viewers pay a predetermined amount of money in order to watch specific programs available only to subscribers of the service. HBO and Showtime are the two oldest and best-known pay services. The fees paid by viewers are usually split fifty-fifty, with half going to the cable system and half to the program supplier.

An effort is being made to provide still another type of funding, referred to as pay-per-view (PPV). In this system, viewers pay a fixed price to watch one specific event. The arithmetic of PPV is intoxicating. Twenty million homes—by no means an unachievable number in television—paying $5 each yields a $100,000,000 take. This is a staggering box office return. But, while the numbers are reachable in theory, there have actually been very few successful events. Again, the reason is buried deep in the psyche of the American people. They seem willing, within limits, to pay only for what they have always paid for—special sports events and movies. There are not many of either available, which may be the definition of the word *special*. In other words, PPV may be a self-limiting concept; this is probably why championship prize fights have been the most notable programs of this kind to date. A recently announced arrangement between Tele-Communications Inc., the nation's largest cable operator, and Carolco Pictures would offer major movies on a PPV basis at the same time as the movies' release in theaters. This would be a serious change in the exhibition-window sequence, in which major movies have always had prior theatrical release. There are several imponderables in the scheme. Is a theatrical box office verification needed to establish the PPV market? Will simultaneous PPV release obliterate the theatrical box office? Or will the two combined exceed the revenues they would generate separately?

For the summer Olympic games held in Barcelona in 1992, the NBC network made an attempt at providing selected sports activities as a pay-per-view event. It was not successful. The story is illustrative of the pitfalls involved in attempting to alter an established tradition in the medium.

NBC had hoped to have at least two million homes agree to pay $125 for the ability to watch all of the Olympic events. This would represent about 5 percent of the approximately forty million homes that had the capacity to receive PPV.

According to an article in the *Wall Street Journal* written during the Barcelona games, NBC and Cablevision, the cable company that was collaborating with NBC on the PPV project, was probably losing over $150 million on the event. NBC had paid $401 million for the rights to telecast the Olympics and invested more than $70 million in production and promotion costs.

What went wrong? For more than three decades, the American viewing public has had the opportunity to enjoy the winter and summer Olympics on free television. As a matter of fact, the worldwide Olympic movement has been underwritten by the rights fees paid by the American television networks. Only their audiences are large enough to support the fees charged by the Olympic Committee. This also means that competitive bidding among the networks has forced up Olympic prices. In 1988, the winter events in Calgary cost ABC $309 million because NBC and CBS were also actively interested. Opening bids began at $275 million. NBC's final bid was $305 million, driving ABC in its relentless pursuit of the rights to $309 million. A post mortem on the financial performances of the games showed that the ABC network lost about $65 million. The only winner financially was the Olympic Committee.

ABC also provided selected college football games for regional PPV in the fall of 1992 (a proposal that was greeted with a great deal of criticism by the ABC affiliates, who saw it as a competitive effort). This attempt at selling individual programs directly to the viewer was less than successful, possibly because college football was readily available on free television.

With respect to the traditional relationships within a network, both the NBC Olympic PPV situation and the ABC college football PPV situation are examples of program decisions made primarily for the financial benefit of the network without considering the effect on the affiliated stations.

There are some troubling philosophic issues concerning PPV as well. To the extent that it tends to transfer programs away from advertiser-supported television, it is economically discriminating, disenfranchising those who are unable to pay. While this effect may be limited, certainly a scenario that presupposes the eventual transfer of something like the NFL or major-league baseball to PPV would be considered a serious loss to the general public. However, this may be academic, since it does not seem likely that pay-per-view will ever be as successful as envisioned by some of its more vocal supporters. In fact, one might argue that pay-per-view already exists on a grand scale under another term, namely *video rentals.*

Despite the interest in PPV, it is still advertising revenues that are the foundation of the American television network system and, consequently, of the Hollywood production process.

Financial support for network television comes from advertising revenues. For obvious reasons, advertisers are keenly interested in the size and nature of the audiences who watch the programs they sponsor (Figure 3–1). The audience reports concerning traditional broadcasting represent the best estimates that can be made of who was watching what and when. However, cable services have been surprisingly successful selling advertising time on a different basis, citing the potential rather than actual audience. There is usually a very large difference between the two. The explanation for this phenomenon seems to lie in the confusion over the meaning of the term *subscriber.* The word has its origins in print, where it means a customer who pays for a specific copy or series of copies of a publication. The presumption is that most of the people who pay for it will read the publication. The word *subscriber* came into use in cable since it, too, represented a monetary transaction of this sort. However, that is where the resemblance ends. It is known that most people buy cable primarily in order to improve the reception of their regular broadcast signals. In the process, they get certain services in the basic package and can add others to that as well.

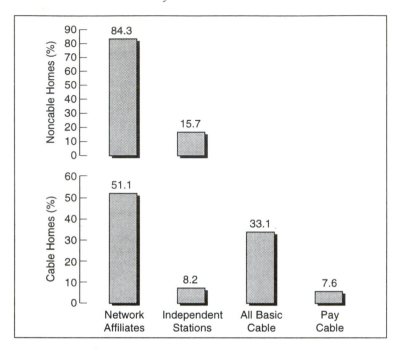

Figure 3.1 1992 Total Day Share (U.S. TV homes = 92,100,000)

For example, the original press stories on the General Electric acquisition of the Financial News Network (FNN)—a cable service—cited the thirty-five million homes that had cable and could receive the service as though this were the FNN market. But in television it is not the potential audience, the subscribers—that is, the homes capable of receiving the service—but the actual audience, the viewers, that equals circulation. At the time of the acquisition, research was already available showing that the actual audience to FNN numbered less than seventy thousand homes. It is obvious that spending over $100 million to reach an audience of this size is not an intelligent risk. (Figure 3–2).

NBC, of course, hoped to expand the original audience and had, as well, expectations about realizing efficiencies of scale relating to its own news organization in its purchase of

FNN. So far, these do not seem to have been realized. In the summer of 1992, NBC announced a $20 million promotional campaign to help boost disappointing ratings. The current prime-time schedule of FNN, now called CNBC, bears no relation to financial news.

Meanwhile, the drain on finances takes money away from NBC's basic network, where an improvement in audience size of one rating point could increase network profits by more than $70 million.

Based on subscribers, the "Big 3" networks have 94,100,000 homes. Still, they are properly measured by actual homes watching specific programs.

To use another familiar example, there are more than fifty-eight million subscribers to CNN, which is part of nearly every

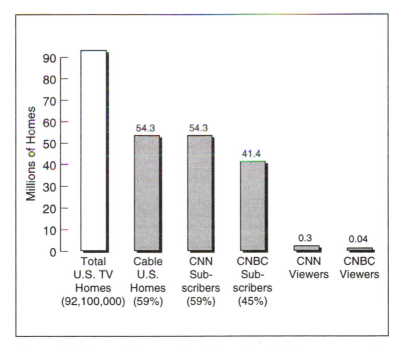

Figure 3.2 Viewers Compared to Subscribers (1992 average = 1/4 hour)

basic cable package. But when Nielsen measures the actual CNN rating, it finds that only a tiny fraction of these people watch. The prime-time rating is 0.6, which means that just over half of 1 percent of these subscribers are watching CNN. The rating for any one of the networks' nightly news broadcasts is well over ten times larger, and there are even local stations whose nightly news broadcasts reach more people. The effect of the word *subscriber* on the purchase of cable advertising time is thus another example of the real effects of psychology in a large-scale business presumably operated on hard-boiled terms.

CBS was not immune to the multichannel virus. It introduced CBS Cable—a "cultural" channel—in the mid-80s. This, too, was an experiment that did not work out.

For its entry into cable, CBS set five objectives: (1) to offer programming that was not readily available on commercial channels; (2) to produce programs that would be perceived to be of high "quality"; (3) to have the schedule comprised of music, dance, drama, and other special artistic endeavors; (4) to keep strict cost controls; and (5) to generate enough sales to more than cover operating costs.

The network succeeded in achieving four of the five goals.

The critics raved about the content. The average cost per hour was low at $2,400. This was due in part to the number of times each episode was rerun. Unfortunately, revenues were not sufficient to cover the costs. Despite prelaunch encouragement, advertisers would not buy time unless actual circulation figures could be provided.

In retrospect, CBS should not have been surprised at the result. PBS, even with the ability to reach many more homes, is continually in financial trouble.

As a percentage of the total population, the number of people who pay admission to museums or concerts or operas is very small—so small that those types of institutions have never been able to support themselves purely on revenues from attendance. The CBS cable channel was designed for very specialized tastes in a medium that, even with all the economies that were in effect, was still very expensive in relation to the circulation. The channel lost $30 million in its last year of existence, and it was estimated that the following year losses would have been about $100 million. There was no profit light at the end of the cultural tunnel.

Before CBS Cable was launched, a great deal of study went into the possibility of introducing a CBS all-news channel. CNN was already in existence and it was known that ABC and Westinghouse were planning a competitive news service. After a detailed evaluation, the idea was scrapped. There were a number of reasons for this.

Costs were a critical issue. It was estimated that CNN then cost about $60 million to operate. CNN employs nonunion personnel as well as a number of college interns, who receive only course credits for their work. Because of union requirements, it would have cost CBS more than $100 million to provide an equivalent service. Furthermore, CNN ratings were very small. Even if a new service made substantial inroads into the CNN audience, neither would have adequate support. In short, CBS concluded that there was, at best, room for one in this field—an evaluation later verified when both ABC and Westinghouse failed in a similar endeavor.

The outsider can look at that second reason and wonder why the audience for a commodity so universally appealing as news could not have been expanded. This, after all, is not a question of sophisticated financial information. Why did the CNN rating represent a limit? Why did CBS not believe it could build enough of an all-news channel following to support its own enterprise?

This brings us to some broader questions about supply and demand in this marketplace. The two basic components of the television marketplace are both limited. One is people, and the other is time. Not only is the total population finite at any given point in time, but the number of that number who watch television is also limited by the demands of their lifestyles—the need to eat, sleep, work, and so forth. All these activities are imprisoned within the most inflexible boundary of all—the twenty-four-hour day.

CBS had to ask itself what would be the likely demand for a second all-news service given these basic limitations and the preexisting availability of news to its potential viewers, which was formidable indeed. On even a single network-affiliated station, something like ten hours of news and information service were already part of the schedule. All viewers had at least three such stations available. In addition, each network had news breaks in their schedules, during both daytime and prime-time hours. Further, in the event of any story of overriding interest, the networks would interrupt regular programming for special coverage. Besides all this, many independent stations in these same localities presented their own news coverage, often at times when the network affiliate was offering entertainment. And none of this took into account the information flowing out through thousands of radio stations or print media.

CNN, in short, was a service designed for a very limited audience, which could not be profitably subdivided. The great resource of CNN is not superior news gathering or news analysis, but airtime. When the super-scale, all-hours news event Desert Storm came along, CNN's ratings increased dramatically. But the CNN ratings after Desert Storm were actually smaller than the ratings that preceded it. As of February 1992, CNN had a .6 rating. The CBS Morning News had a 2.6 rating. The CBS Evening News had a 9.6 rating. That is to say, CBS was reaching over four times as many viewers in the morning and over 16 times as many in the evening as CNN.

How, then, does CNN exist? On a .6 rating it could not survive solely on advertising revenues. It has two other revenue streams. One is the fees it receives from the cable systems that carry it. The other is its international distribution. Even so, the nonunion cost aspect is probably still crucial to its financial result and continued viability.

Of course, *subsidy* is a word that can be applied to much of cable. Cable began its life as a service called CATV. It was just what it said it was—a superantenna that brought a clear picture to under-serviced areas. People bought cable to improve their reception of regular, over-the-air programming. In fact, to this day, an improved signal is the dominant reason for buying cable, and, to this day, more viewing is done of the traditional broadcast services, in cable homes, than of all other services combined (Table 3–1).

The "must carry" rules obliged cable systems to carry all of the channels already available in a given area. From the cable point of view, this proved to be one of the most benign pieces of legislation in communications history, since cable operators thereby acquired $6 or $7 billion worth of product at no cost, for which they could in turn charge their customers.

All of these situations have at their core the question of the viewers' psyche, that endlessly fascinating and often surprising x-factor in the medium. Consider this: in 1992, after more than a dozen years of audience research, Nielsen reported that 65 percent of all the viewing in a cable-equipped home is of the commercial channels carried by the cable system. Just as some people are willing to pay for a gallon of water even when perfectly safe tap water is available to them, viewers in cable-equipped homes are paying to watch free, over-the-air commercial stations because of improved reception. What they may not understand is that, thanks to the "must carry" rules, the cable companies pay nothing for the programming that provides the bulk of their appeal. It is difficult to think of any other industry in which this situation occurs, and it is now being challenged. The Federal Communications Commission in early 1993 issued a decision that allows for retransmission fees. The cable companies have taken the position that if they are

TABLE 3–1. Top Cable Programs, April 12–18, 1992

| | HHs. (000) | Rtg. | Program | Time (ET) | Netw |
|---|---|---|---|---|---|
| 1. | 2,657 | 4.4 | Death Train (movie) | Wed. 9–11p | US |
| 2. | 2,586 | 4.2 | L.A. Verdict Coverage | Sat. 10–10:30a | CN |
| 3. | 2,367 | 4.0 | Sea Wolf (movie) | Sun. 8–10p | TN |
| 4. | 2,131 | 3.5 | Style | Sat. 10:30–10:45a | CN |
| 5. | 2,119 | 3.5 | Pro Boxing | Tue. 9–11p | US |
| 6. | 2,057 | 3.4 | Monday Night Raw | Mon. 9–11p | US |
| 7. | 2,049 | 3.4 | Murder, She Wrote | Wed. 8–9p | US |
| 8. | 2,008 | 3.3 | L.A. Verdict Coverage | Sat. 10:45–11a | CN |
| 9. | 1,947 | 3.2 | L.A. Verdict Coverage | Sat. 11–11:30a | CN |
| 10. | 1,902 | 3.1 | Midway (part 2) (movie) | Sat. 10–11:45p | TE |
| 11. | 1,809 | 2.9 | NASCAR Racing | Sun. 1–4p | ESF |
| 12. | 1,800 | 3.1 | Ren & Stimpy | Sun. 11–11:30a | NIC |
| 13. | 1,795 | 2.9 | MLB (Pirates v. Dodgers) | Sun. 8–11:20p | ESF |
| 14. | 1,787 | 2.9 | Smokey and the Bandit II (movie) | Sun. 10:30a–12:45p | TE |
| 15. | 1,778 | 2.9 | MLB (Cubs v. Braves) | Tue. 7:30–10;30p | TE |
| 16. | 1,744 | 2.9 | Murder, She Wrote | Mon. 8–9p | US |
| 17. | 1,712 | 2.8 | Murder, She Wrote | Tue. 8–9p | US |
| 18. | 1,672 | 2.8 | Murder, She Wrote | Fri. 8–9p | US |
| 19. | 1,647 | 2.8 | Ren & Stimpy | Sat. 9–9:30p | NIC |
| 20. | 1,618 | 2.8 | Rugrats | Sun. 10:30–11a | NIC |
| 21. | 1,613 | 2.7 | MLB (Braves v. Giants) | Sun. 4–8:30p | TE |
| 22. | 1,555 | 2.6 | Over the Top (movie) | Sat. 4–6p | TE |
| 23. | 1,527 | 2.5 | MLB (Orioles v. Rangers) | Wed. 8:30–12m | ESF |
| 24. | 1,524 | 2.6 | Clarissa Explains It All | Sat. 8–8:30p | NIC |
| 25. | 1,522 | 2.6 | Shadow Riders (movie) | Sun. 6–8p | TN |
| 26. | 1,503 | 2.5 | Fletch Lives (movie) | Thu. 9–11p | US |
| 27. | 1,485 | 2.5 | Breaker! Breaker! (movie) | Sun. 12:45–2:30p | TE |
| 28. | 1,463 | 2.4 | MLB (Cubs v. Braves) | Mon 7:30–10:15p | TE |
| 29. | 1,435 | 2.4 | Sea Wolf (movie) | Sun. 10–12m | TN |
| 30. | 1,427 | 2.4 | Rugrats | Sat. 7:30–8p | NIC |
| 31. | 1,415 | 2.3 | Silk Stockings | Sun. 11–12m | US |
| 32. | 1,413 | 2.3 | Death Train (movie) | Sun. 8–10p | US |
| 33. | 1,394 | 2.3 | Kung Fu (movie) | Sun. 2:30–4p | TE |
| 34. | 1,389 | 2.3 | Once Bitten (movie) | Sun. 2–4p | US |
| 35. | 1,380 | 2.2 | Money Week | Sat. 9:30–10a | CN |
| 36. | 1,365 | 2.3 | Roundhouse | Sat. 8:30–9p | NIC |
| 37. | 1,364 | 2.3 | Salute Shorts | Sun. 11:30–12n | NIC |
| 38. | 1,353 | 2.3 | Are You Afraid of the Dark? | Sat. 9:30–10p | NIC |

TABLE 3–1. (Continued)

| HHs. (000) | Rtg. | Program | Time (ET) | Network |
|---|---|---|---|---|
| 39. 1,334 | 2.3 | The Statler Brothers | Sat. 9–10p | TNN |
| 40. 1,330 | 2.2 | Sportscenter | Sun. 11:20p–12:21a | ESPN |

The above are the top 40 basic cable programs, ranked by total number of households tuning in. Ratings are based on each network's total coverage households at the time of the program. Data are supplied by outside sources based on Nielsen Media Research.

obliged to pay for the privilege of carrying the commercial stations, they will pass the cost on to their customers and declare it to be a rate hike forced by the commercial broadcasters, who have paid for the programming in the first place.

During the summer of 1993, the three major networks carried on a serious effort to convince the cable operators that unless fees were paid they would not allow their programs to be carried. The fact that the three networks took this position appeared to strengthen the resolve of affiliated stations around the country. Then the ABC Network broke ranks and unilaterally decided that it was in its interest to provide its programs to cable systems in exchange for a basic cable channel that ABC would program. The content of this new channel would consist of sports-related programs and be called ESPN2. Once ABC decided to give away its valuable programming, NBC soon made a similar decision. CBS, shortly thereafter, also conceded to cable pressure.

These moves contain all the elements of a serious misjudgment that will accrue to the benefit of the cable industry. The broadcasters gave away their product, easily the most attractive in the field, for the chance to create another channel with very limited appeal, that will be costly to program and for which the cable companies again, will not have to pay. Score two more points for the cable industry and zero points for the networks!

It is possible to speculate about a reversal of this history— in which the traditional station does not exist but the rest of

television as we know it today does. Then along comes someone with the idea of providing first-run entertainment, live
local and national news and information, and live play-by-play
coverage of professional and collegiate sports, at no charge.

The idea certainly sounds extravagant. It would have to
include the Hollywood soundstages and the back lots and the
locations where entertainment was being created. It would
have to include just about every city and town in America and
arenas, stadiums, and playing fields all around them. It would
have to provide for the gathering of news in all of those places
as well as around the globe. It would have to be able to knit all
this together into a continuous schedule planned out weeks
and months in advance. It would have to seek out advertisers,
local and national, establish rates acceptable to them, and arrange for their commercials to be inserted where and when
they wanted them. It would require billions of dollars, thousands and thousands of employees, an intricate chain of hardware linking America to itself and the world with second-by-
second efficiency. The concept seems mind-boggling in its
complexity and its ambitions. Yet it exists. Perhaps the real
point is that no system of any consequence would have developed in the first place had it not been for the half-century of
steady investment and development by the original entrepreneurs, the broadcasters.

Cable came into being with this system in place. With that
as a base, cable went through a period of rapid expansion.
There was enormous growth in circulation and in revenues.
One unforeseen consequence of this is already apparent—a
gradual reversal of the supportive legislative and regulatory
atmosphere that prevailed in cable's early days. Whereas cable
was initially encouraged as a means of improving services,
making the industry more competitive and reining in the all-
powerful networks, it is now being seen as an industry that has
imposed its own unjustified demands on a defenseless consumer. New legislation replaces the old "must carry" rules

with a marketplace system in which broadcasters and cable systems will bargain over carrying broadcasters' signals.

The new legislation could expose a weakness in the cable position. The free ride on network product has allowed cable to get by with a severely underfinanced production capacity. If cable ever has to either buy that product or produce some equivalent, it is likely to be thrown severely off balance. Despite this, the race to add channels goes on. It might be called an example of a supply-side economy without the supply.

### How the Market Works

Cable advertising time and broadcast advertising time have the characteristics of a commodity. That is, there is a fixed quantity—in this case, the total number of advertising positions—but the demand for it is flexible. In these circumstances, it is very important that the sales department be able to forecast demand accurately in order to obtain optimum prices. The definition of optimum prices is to have inventory sold out when advertising dollars in the market are fully expended. It is almost as embarrassing for sales managers to allow inventory to be sold out at prices that are too low, with money still in the market, as it is to be unsold when the market dries up.

The two most commonly negotiated sales fall into categories referred to as *up-front* and *scatter*. As the term implies, up-front means a commitment before the fact—sales made during the summer months for schedules that will begin with the new season. They are usually for twenty-six or fifty-two weeks, with firm prices agreed to for the duration of the order. Scatter prices are for schedules of a short duration in programs that are already running, primarily any order less than thirteen weeks. The great guessing game between network sales departments and client agencies is whether the demand for advertising time will be weak or strong at a given point in the future. Demand determines whether the later scatter market prices will be higher or lower than the earlier up-front prices. And that is where strategy enters the situation.

Pricing obviously affects total network revenues, but it also plays a role in the cancellation of individual programs, since the acceptable price in the market may not be sufficient to cover a given program's costs even when the ratings are respectable. This usually occurs when overall ratings, and ratings against certain special audience segments, are markedly different. There are two interesting examples of how this can work, one old and one recent. In 1969, CBS had three very highly rated programs that were difficult to sell at prices that would cover the cost of production. Red Skelton, Jackie Gleason, and Ed Sullivan all had above-average audience circulations. When the agents for Red Skelton demanded more money for the star, since the program was already not generating enough sales for success, the program was canceled. The reason given to Skelton was "demographics". While his audience may have been large, most of the viewers were over fifty years of age, and most advertisers were looking for an audience of predominantly eighteen- to forty-nine-year-olds. This was a case of pricing that was not justified against a specific advertising target group.

In 1992, NBC canceled three programs also because of demographics. Programs starring Carroll O'Connor, Andy Griffith, and the "Golden Girls" were dropped, as NBC tried to attract more eighteen- to forty-nine-year-old viewers.

The hazard here for a network is in accepting lower overall circulation even when an immediate financial gain is involved. The decisions in 1969 were based on financial needs of the network with little regard for the viewers. The replacement programs did not perform as well as the ones replaced. And, twenty years later, CBS was struggling with the same age-demographic issue. In the more recent example, two of the NBC programs were picked up; one by CBS and one by ABC, in the belief that those shows would add audience to their respective schedules. As of 1994, both *Matlock* and *In the Heat of the Night* were still in the schedules.

Demographics have been a network sales issue for many years. Over time, efforts have been undertaken to demonstrate that there is substantial value in the audience that is fifty years of age or older. There is a large body of supportive research on this topic, but it is not documentation, but rather negotiation that is the issue. Advertisers have discovered that by negotiating prices on the basis of the eighteen- to forty-nine-year-old viewers, in actual performance the advertiser will reach the 50-plus viewer also. If the value of the 50-plus audience is recognized by the advertiser, it only means the clients will pay more. There is also a contrary body of opinion that holds that in the long run, negotiating on a fragment of the audience—any fragment—is a mistake for advertisers, since it narrows supply and therefore concentrates demand—the last thing a buyer should want. What the networks need to do is change their sales approach. They need new marketing ideas and new sales techniques.

Most advertisers understand that successful advertising requires three things: reach, frequency, and impact.

For more than fifty years, advertising purchases have measured efficiency on a cost-per-thousand basis, that is, the price paid to reach one thousand potential customers. This amount is computed by dividing the audience into the cost of the advertising time. If an advertiser pays $400,000 for a commercial spot, and it reaches ten million homes, he is paying $4 for each thousand homes reached. This approach measures reach and frequency, but it does not consider impact—a far more difficult dimension to quantify. It is obvious that cheaper does not necessarily mean better. In the early days of television, most advertisers were sole sponsors of specific programs, such as Westinghouse and *Studio One, General Electric Theater, The Alcoa Hour, Armstrong Circle Theater, The U.S. Steel Hour, The Texaco Star Theater, The Kraft Music Hall,* and so on. Full sponsorship of early television programs was effective. As the cost of television advertising grew, advertisers began to exchange impact for an effort to reach more viewers more frequently with more and shorter announcements. It may very well be that in a time of multiple channels and audience fragmentation, current advertisers should make greater efforts toward improving the impact of their messages, by returning to full or partial sponsorships of programs. This is not easily done, since costs now make it virtually impossible for a single advertiser to sponsor a weekly program. And, in many cases, the sheer quantity of brands requiring exposure makes this far too limited a platform. Advertisers like Hallmark and General Electric, concentrating on corporate image, still sponsor programs, on a highly selective basis, and seem to benefit highly.

As television moves toward the year 2000, the American population will not have enough time or money to use all the options available for leisure-time activities. Neither will advertisers. The businesses that will succeed are those that will pay greater attention to innovative marketing techniques.

Ultimately, just as in any other business in a free market, the total revenues generated by the network sales department have to be sufficient to cover the cost of the entire enterprise. The problem arises because the cost-revenue burden is never evenly distributed across the entire schedule. Weak programs that fail to cover the cost of production need to be subsidized by more successful programs. One-time, low-rated specials scheduled for reasons of enhancing a quality image or as a public service need support from more popular endeavors. Basically, total revenues will always be the result of total circulation. If a network attempts to program to a specific, limited segment of audience as radio does, limited circulation will be the result. Again, limited circulation means limited income; limited income means limited capacity to compete for product.

In the last analysis, superior circulation is the networks' trump card. A network that begins to turn away from programming for mass audiences is on the road to self-destruction.

Although advertisers pay the networks a price for commercial time based on circulation, the specific price for a certain program can be affected by the laws of supply and demand. When advertisers' demand is heavy, prices may rise much higher than the consumer price index would seem to justify. Needless to say, that is when advertisers can become quite disturbed. During his eleven years as president of the broadcasting activities of CBS, Gene had many meetings with the advertisers. Most often they were pleasant ones, but not always. In 1984, the chairman and chief executive officer of Procter & Gamble, the network's largest advertiser, John Smale, asked for a special meeting to discuss a very important topic. The word *important* was superfluous in this case: anything on the mind of the head of Procter & Gamble was important to CBS.

The discussion that took place centered on the cost of network advertising time. At a time when his company was attempting to lower its overall operating costs, Mr. Smale was extremely upset that the price increases for network television advertising time were in double digits. An hour was spent discussing supply and demand for advertising time. Gene explained how commercial time was sold as a commodity that reflected the strength or weakness of the advertising market. As it happened, 1984 was a very strong advertising year, due to additional advertising pressure from election-year political ads and Olympic Games advertising. Because of the economic conditions and CBS's strong audience ratings, the broadcasting activities that year generated over $400 million in profits on revenues of $2.7 billion. This was the most profitable year in the broadcasting history of CBS, including 1993.

The point Gene made was that, unlike P & G, which could keep its plants producing bars of a successful soap product at a static price, CBS had a limited amount of fixed inventory, and market pressure was released through higher prices. The formula is simple: Flexible amounts of inventory can mean fixed prices and low increases. Fixed amounts of inventory mean flexible prices and possibly large increases, or possibly decreases.

This was also the year that the president of the Ford Motor Company for North America, Harold "Red" Poling, wanted to discuss the increasing costs of network television. Ford was requesting all of their suppliers to keep cost growth to a minimum. Since the network was a supplier of advertising time, it too should keep increases down.

Mr. Poling invited some of the senior CBS executives to Detroit to see the Ford long-range plan that had been presented to the Ford Board of Directors and to its employees. One statement in the presentation stood out among all others: it was possible for Japan to deliver a similar-sized automobile in downtown Detroit for $2,500 less than Ford could. Detroit, of course, was Ford's home city. While most of this difference was due to expenditures for labor, Ford wanted their suppliers to help absorb the added costs. We had to point out that the network was hardly a supplier in the sense that units of the Ford manufacturing and distribution process were, and that in any case we could not manufacture more time. What we had was available for sale, and the demand for it determined the prices. Our concern was not the price of a car delivered in downtown Detroit, but the price of keeping the network delivering maximum audiences.

Not surprisingly, neither P & G nor Ford was happy with the outcome of these discussions. Unfortunately, the network had no alternative solution to the problem.

It is believed that it was in reaction to network pricing in a strong marketplace that a number of major advertisers began to buy low-rated, low-priced ad spots on cable systems, in place of the more costly, though more efficient, network commercials. In the long run, this action is self-defeating. Ten commercials with a one rating do not equal one commercial with a ten rating. They reach fewer total viewers, and the logistics of purchasing the announcements, as well as monitoring their performance, is much more confusing and much more costly. The result of a less efficient approach to advertising expenditures is fewer sales—an outcome that is not healthy for the client, the network, or the country. Ultimately, advertisers and their agencies will need ways to "remassify" the audience if the clients hope to improve marketing and sales efficiencies. If not, with lower volume, profit improvements of manufacturers can only come with higher consumer prices. Logic, therefore, would indicate a continuing need by advertisers for networks capable of reaching virtually all of the television homes in the country.

Whenever the networks try to address the ad pricing problem from the inventory side, by adding commercial time, they are accused of producing "clutter" and weakening the effectiveness of each advertisement. Also, their affiliated stations complain that the added commercials result in money going to the network that used to go to the stations.

Whatever the effects of clutter might be on the performance of commercials, there is no doubt that it is a favorite negotiating weapon for advertisers. The line goes: "if you add more spots I will pay less, and I will spend the money I save someplace else; I will buy more cable advertising." The fact that magazines, cable, and independent stations have more advertising clutter than the networks does not prevent clients from spending millions of dollars at high costs per person reached in these media.

In the broadcast sense clutter would include all material not related to the "story." This would be commercials, promotions for other programs, and full credits, which name those people associated with the program (that is, cast of performers, producers, writers, and so on). Clearly, this definition raises other issues in regard to perceived clutter. For example, the time allotted to credits has grown as the list of names associated with a program has increased. One need only compare a half-hour program of twenty years ago with a contemporary half-hour program. The longer list today is also a factor in why the costs of production have escalated over time. However, credits do not affect network income.

Other non-program elements do. Commercials are necessary for obvious reasons. Promotional announcements are the networks' advertising for future programs in an effort to increase the ratings, and, thereby, the revenues of promoted shows. These announcements are necessary to increase the value of network programs. They are also one of the benefits of advertising on network television. As stated earlier, while individual programs come and go, the schedule lasts. There is an advantage to advertising in programs that receive promotional announcements. It is the complete schedule and the promotion of it that attract audiences that ultimately benefit the advertisers. *60 Minutes* would not attract an audience as large as it does if it were distributed by satellite directly to TV homes without the benefit of association with the local affiliate and the enormous promotional effort it is given across the networks' schedule.

It is interesting to note that clutter is seldom used in regard to newspapers and magazines. The most successful publications are those that are praised for having the largest number of ad pages. The more successful the magazine becomes, the more advertising it attracts. Essentially, what advertisers choose to call clutter is simply content, and it should be judged on that basis. If broadcasters accept the idea that it is a separate and somehow pejorative category, they do themselves a disservice.

Television rates for commercial time had their origin in radio. As television began to evolve, advertisers discovered the unique quality of motion added to words, and the impact that resulted from the combination. Next to a salesperson in a face-to-face situation, TV advertising became the most effective sales tool for moving goods and services. Nonetheless, the economics did not evolve parallel with the effectiveness. This happened because even though television had much more impact than radio as an advertising vehicle, television began life tied to the advertisers' rate base for radio. Advertisers, accustomed to the economics of radio, paid only a small premium for the "pictures." This story is an example of the weight of psychology in a marketplace situation. Television rates were viewed in terms of the degree of increase over radio rates. Advertising budgets could not be revised overnight. Only a certain level of increase could be tolerated. Because of this, television in the 1990s is still less expensive for equal circulation than print advertising. In 1992, it was estimated that newspaper advertising amounted to $33 billion and all television advertising was $28 billion. Nevertheless, tradition, habits, statistics, and conventional wisdom are sometimes overridden by a single, overpowering creative idea, such as the following.

One morning, when Gene was director of sales for WCBS-TV in New York City, which liked to call itself the largest television station in the world, he received a telephone call from a stranger. The caller told Gene he was planning to spend millions of dollars in advertising in New York and would reveal his plans if Gene would meet him in Room 1105 of the Roosevelt Hotel that afternoon. With some trepidation but much more curiosity Gene agreed. When he knocked on the door, it was opened by a thin man with hawklike features who invited him in. The room was very small. The only piece of furniture was a double bed that almost filled the entire space. The man sat down on one corner, and Gene sat on the other. The man then proceeded to tell how he planned to put a brand-name on a previously unbranded product; a well-known, everyday, natural product that could not be "produced." This was an unheard-of strategy, and it seemed the height of futility. He wanted the name of a medium-sized, good advertising agency to help him. His story was unique, his style strange, but in time, he was successful. And that was how Gene first met Frank Perdue, "a tough man" who gave a brand-name to chickens. Scali, McCabe and Sloves was the advertising agency on the Perdue account. Their creative use of television quickly established the name Perdue Chickens in the New York City area. It is doubtful that any other medium would have been so effective so fast.

### Distribution—Critical and Unique

The network's potential advertising revenue is directly affected by the local affiliates. If they do not clear a program, the audience to the network show in that market is lost and with it that share of advertising revenue. The network-affiliate relationship is critical and unique, as this story illustrates.

Key Largo, Florida, in November of 1977. All Gene knew about Key Largo came from the John Huston movie, a film noir as it would now be called, dark, brooding, a study of corruption, natural and human. Bogart and Bacall; Claire Trevor; Edward G. Robinson in a tub; fierce tropical storms; thick fog; and shadowy interiors in a decaying Gothic hotel.

The Ocean Reef Club bore no resemblance to this. It glittered in the reflection of its own lagoon, complete with pet dolphins. Ocean-going yachts were tied up at its private dock. Outside the main channel was the largest underwater park in the United States, one of the most frequented diving destinations in the world.

There was one similarity between what Bogart, Bacall, and company were doing in Key Largo and why Gene was there: both situations involved a transfer of power. In the movie, the means of transfer is counterfeit money, which is to restore ex-gangster Robinson to his former glory. In Gene's case, the meeting came about because there had been a wholesale change in the management of CBS's broadcasting activities, of

William S. Paley, founder of CBS after receiving a silver tray from affiliated stations for his efforts on their behalf. With Gene Jankowski (*left*) and Charles Brakefield (*right*), former chairman of the CBS affiliate board.
*Source:* CBS Inc.

which he was now the head. The new management team was at Ocean Reef for its first formal meeting with the Affiliate Advisory Board—the group who represented the two hundred-plus stations that carried the CBS Television Network's programming.

The meeting was to be significant for another reason, too. William S. Paley, founder, chairman, and chief executive officer of CBS would attend. This was a rarity. His presence was of course an emphatic personal endorsement of the new management team. But it also testified to the nature of the broadcasting system for which that team was responsible. Without the support of the stations the Affiliate Advisory Board represented, there could be no CBS Television Network, for these stations were not owned by CBS. They were owned and operated by a wide variety of corporations and individuals spread all across the nation. And it was the stations, not the network, who were licensed to broadcast by the Federal Communications Commission. They had the absolute right to accept or reject any programming offered to them by CBS. So the meeting at Key Largo was a cameo of the special nature of broadcasting in America, the only country with an interweaving of national and local sources in a unique economic and communications interdependence.

There was another factor, not immediately apparent, and perhaps even obscured by the elegance of the surroundings. This was a business that had been built from the ground up, by individuals, one station at a time. Its original roots were local, and it had never lost them. There were men at that meeting who had obtained the earliest broadcast licenses issued in America; there were even some who had been on the air before that. In a business that had grown to acquire the heaviest creative burden ever experienced by any medium, there was simultaneously a deeply practical cast.

No one knew better than William S. Paley what these stations meant to CBS. He had started courting stations in 1927 and he had never stopped. They were his outlets, his connection with the customers—first listeners, in radio, and then viewers, in television. He gave the stations programming; they gave him presence in every city, town, and hamlet in America.

It was a cooperative enterprise, based on mutual interest. Together he and they prospered—or failed. If their local programming and his national service attracted audiences that advertisers would pay to reach, both won. If not, they both went out of business. The tastes and styles might vary from community to community, but the issue was always the same— they had to connect with the needs and interests of the folks out there to survive. Broadcasting in America was private enterprise, and therefore it was market-driven; that is to say, it had to respond to demand. This separated it from most of the other systems in the world, which were government-owned and driven by commands flowing down from superiors, not up from users.

The network-affiliate system was unique in another sense as well. The stations were not just outlets; they were also suppliers. Their local programming was a vital part of the total service. This was especially true of their news and public affairs activities. Each station provided coverage of local events; this became a complement to the national and international news coverage of the network. What eventually emerged was a remarkable mosaic—a service with several hundred local origination points coupled with worldwide capabilities.

Thus, while the word *network* in its nationwide sense became the dominant image of the total service, what it actually meant at the level of the user was that he or she could find out what the mayor did that day, what the weather was likely to be, or what the high school football scores were—all at the same place on the dial that carried what the President was up to, NFL games, and what happened in Tokyo, Bonn, or Cairo. This system reflects the political, economic, and social patterns of America, which is not surprising, since it grew out of them.

This omnibus concept of service was to prove critical as the networks entered the 1980s. Viewers accustomed to as few as seven channels found themselves with ten, then twenty, then fifty. The network share of the market did decline, but the networks did not disappear, nor are they likely to, since their concept of service is still unique and is still preferred above all the others.

The service is unique because it draws upon the multiple

resources provided by more than two hundred stations—each its own program source—plus the single concentrated resource of the network. The combination can and does invest far more in product than any of its rivals. The part that comes as a surprise to many outsiders is that the networks pay the stations to carry their programs. The first time Gene went to Washington, D.C., as the new head of the CBS broadcasting activities to meet with various officials and talk about network television, he was amazed at how little they knew about network procedures. Most of them believed that the affiliated stations paid the network for the programs they carried. While the uninitiated may consider network compensation a cost, in reality it is an investment. For approximately $150 million in station payments, each network, ABC, CBS, and NBC, has the right to sell billions of dollars' worth of station commercial inventory. This process was developed by William Paley during the 1930's. It was a sensible system. The stations received top-quality programs that they could not afford to produce themselves, and the networks received guaranteed advertising time that could be sold to national clients. All parts of the system benefited from this arrangement.

Some stations are more dominant in each city than others, thereby providing a competitive advantage. CBS, having more leading stations affiliated with its network, has historically paid more compensation than any of the other networks. Many of the broadcast pioneers signed up as CBS affiliated at the beginning of network television, and they and the networks grew together. We cite some of them here in the spirit of a line from Stephen Vincent Benet's wonderful poem about American place-names: "I have fallen in love with American names," he wrote. These names, from Kalamazoo to Spartanburg, from Providence to Seattle, and hundreds more, are their own best testimony to the geography that is a network.

Affiliated with the network, CBS had stations like KOOL-TV Phoenix; WBT Charlotte, N.C.; WWL-TV New Orleans;

WCAX-TV Burlington, Vt.; WTIC-TV (WSFB) Hartford, Conn.; WREC-TV Memphis; KSL-TV Salt Lake City; KIRO-TV Seattle; WCCO-TV Minneapolis; WKZO-TV Kalamazoo, Mich.; KZTV Corpus Christi, Tex.; WCMO-TV Kansas City, Mo.; WHAS-TV Louisville, Ky.; WKRG-TV Mobile, Ala.; WRAL-TV Raleigh-Durham, N.C.; WJXT-TV Jacksonville, Fla.; and WSPA-TV Spartanburg, S.C.

The other, older networks also have their share of solid affiliates. Among the NBC stations that performed very well included WBZ-TV Boston; KSDK-TV St. Louis; WLWT Cincinnati; WJAR-TV Providence, R.I.; WMSV-TV Nashville; and KING-TV Seattle. Outstanding ABC stations include WSB-TV Atlanta; WHAS-TV Louisville, Ky.; WCVB-TV Boston; WXYZ-TV Detroit; and WFAA-TV Dallas. These were dominant stations early on, known for having strong signals and strong community ties. As a result, over time, realizing the value these stations brought to the network, the networks paid to keep them in the lineup. This system worked well for more than fifty years.

While it may not be surprising that laypersons are ignorant of the network-affiliate compensation arrangements, it is unexpected that recently the networks themselves seem to have lost sight of the reasons for it. In 1992, the management of CBS told its affiliates compensation would be cut substantially—a position from which it later, at least temporarily, retreated. Eventually, the network hopes to eliminate compensation completely. The argument is that if the network programs add value to the stations, the stations should pay the network for the right to carry them.

There are a number of problems with this position. First, the stations are the licencees. They have the absolute right to reject any program for any reason and to seek programs elsewhere. If compensation is cut or eliminated, it can only encourage them to do so. This is not an idle threat. Program production has been growing for more than a decade, and it is expected that new sources for alternative programming will continue to develop during the 1990s. Second, there is the question of leverage. The three networks today have virtually total clearance—through their affiliates, they can reach 98 percent of the television homes in America. This is a unique advantage. No other technology can match this level of penetration. But even a small loss—10 to 15 percent—can be calamitous. That means the stations need drop only three hours of prime time to do major damage to the network. It would be tragic if, having fought off major competition for more than a decade, the only serious damage to the networks is self-inflicted. Lack of clearances inevitably leads to a loss of viewers, and that in turn leads to a loss of revenues. Lower clearances would automatically become one of the elements at work in the so-called erosion of network audiences.

Then, in the spring of 1994 the largest affiliate shift in network history occurred. CBS affiliates located in Detroit, Cleveland, Tampa, Milwaukee, Phoenix, Atlanta, and other important cities switched affiliations, and the "war" for stations was officially on. As a result of earlier short-sighted decisions, the three networks eventually paid more than 150 million dollars in additional compensation to hold on to their station lineups.

The question of network erosion is, itself, another example of the underlying complexity of the network business. Numerous newspaper and magazine articles have been written about it, and each year brings more articles on the same topic. The usual reference points are the size of the audience that watched network programs in 1980 and the size of the audience in the current season. In this thirteen-year time span, a vast number of events occurred that need to be considered when any such comparison is done. One element that is not usually considered is the number of news programs in prime time that have been introduced during that period. Another element is the passing of the Prime Time Access Rule mentioned earlier, whereby network affiliates in the fifty largest cities are not permitted to broadcast off-network programs in prime time. This rule has resulted in smaller audience lead-ins to network programs as well as larger audiences for independent competitors. Another occurrence, as already discussed, is the genesis of the Fox Television Network.

In regard to the news element, in 1980, there was only one regularly scheduled prime-time news hour. In 1992, there were at least five, and if reality-type shows are included there were eighteen. These were *60 Minutes, Rescue 911, 20/20, Unsolved Mysteries, Prime Time Live, 48 Hours, America's Funniest Home Videos, America's Funniest People, How'd They Do That?, Street Stories, American Detective, Dateline NBC, Day One, Top Cops, FBI-Untold Stories, I Witness Video,* and *Miracles and Other Wonders.* And there were more promised for the 1993–94 season. The lower cost to produce a news hour helped to bring this about. The licensing fee paid by a network for an entertainment hour averages about $1 million, even though the actual cost of production may be substantially higher. It is possible for a news hour to be produced for as little as $250,000. This relationship, however, can be deceiving. While a program produced by a news division may be inexpensive when compared to the cost of a prime-time entertainment hour, it is almost certain that the rating of the news program will be much lower than that of the entertainment program. To illustrate, in 1990 CBS entertainment programming averaged a 12 rating and a 28 percent share while its news hours averaged a 9.5 rating and 16 percent share. For NBC, the respective numbers were a 13.2 rating and 22 percent share for entertainment and a 7.7 rating and 12 percent share for the news hours. For ABC, the numbers were 12.5 rating and 21 percent share for entertainment and 11.7 rating and 21 percent share for its news hours. What it comes down to is that a loss in circulation of around 33 percent is being offset by a drop of costs that will probably be at least 50 percent. That's certainly sound business arithmetic on the face of it, but there is a problematic side: the loss in potential. While entertainment programs often fail, they are the only ones capable of achieving the maximum circulation available in the medium (with a single exception, *60 Minutes*), and circulation is still the networks' trump card.

Other than cost considerations, there is another reason the networks favor ownership. That is the possibility of additional revenues from future sales. But that is a faulty assumption. In running a network, it is not pride of authorship, but success of product that should be the most important consideration. It is unwise to believe that any one place has a lock on creative success. No single studio has ever had it; no single producer has ever had it; there is no reason to think that a network is going to magically eliminate the historic ratios of failure in creative work just by putting it all under one roof. In fact, the odds are in the opposite direction. At a network, business runs on circulation, not production. It needs the best ideas from the best people and should not care where they come from. And Hollywood, being what it is, there is a very good chance that those ideas will come from the studios. That is history.

The risk-reward relationship on the entertainment side becomes public when the time comes to renew a big hit. CBS pays a large premium to Angela Lansbury, the star of *Murder, She Wrote,* in order to keep this enormously successful program on the air. Without her, the program is at risk; without the program, the CBS Sunday night lineup is at risk; and without that lineup, a leadership position is at risk. As a footnote here, it can be said that there is no better bargaining position than that of a hit show at the front end of a lineup. In a sense, *Murder She Wrote* is in an even better position because it is preceded by *60 Minutes.*

*60 Minutes* is probably the most phenomenal program in the medium's history and the most notable exception to the news-versus-entertainment rating issue. It has provided a supercharged springboard for the network's Sunday lineup for twenty-two years. Even better, it is owned by CBS—so there is no production company to bargain with. Thus *Murder, She Wrote* is in the enviable position of being both powerfully supported and supportive. It is tucked in behind a juggernaut, and, coming at eight o'clock, two more hours are dependent on its performance. *The Cosby Show* was, in a sense, the equivalent of *60 Minutes,* or *Murder, She Wrote* for NBC on Thursday. Those power lead-off situations are the biggest bargaining chips in the business. On the other hand, with five news hours now replacing entertainment, the networks have lost an opportunity for more blockbuster programming to be developed in a highly competitive environment.

Another important factor that affected the "big 3" network ratings between 1980 and 1992 was the creation of the Fox Network. In 1980 the three major networks had a combined prime-time audience share of 85 percent. At that time it was predicted that with the advent of various cable systems and more independent stations, the networks' share would drop below 60 percent by 1990 and would continue to decline after that—that is, if the three networks were even still around. In that climate nobody expected a new network would come along. The perceived wisdom was that the whole network idea was a thing of the past, a behemoth lumbering toward extinction. But Fox did appear, and it prospered, even though it does not yet have the full national coverage of its older rivals. Since the debate was not really about the number of networks, but the viability of the network concept, the issue today is the combined performance of the four networks in the markets where all four are in operation. In those markets the networks' prime-time share in the 1990–91 season was 74 percent. Not only is the network idea alive and well, but, clearly, Fox, an old-fashioned kind of competitor, has had a bigger impact on ABC, CBS, and NBC than all of cable combined. This hard evidence from the marketplace supports the thesis that the networks will not succumb to outside forces.

In this chapter we have dealt mainly with the business of television—the hard facts of supply and demand, costs and revenues, and the interlocking progression of production, distribution, and funding that drives the medium. In the next chapter we will enter an area where this business deals not with imagined or created materials but with the stuff of reality—news.

# Chapter *4*

## Television and Washington

Three factors—news, an activity; Washington, a place; and the trust of the public—compose what we term *the credibility triangle*. Washington is both the chief source of news and the regulatory power for television. Broadcasters report on Washington, more often than not in a manner not wholly agreeable to those in power, and are at the same time beholden to it for their licenses and for the rules that govern their business. On the other hand, television is regarded as pivotal in the process that is of greatest interest in Washington: getting elected. So there is both dependency and contention in the relationship; it is both confrontational and collegial. What tends to keep these two contradictory factors in place is the presence of a third factor. Neither government nor news can function without an underpinning of public trust, and a large measure of that trust is invested in the public's perception of how the two relate— how the press treats the government and how the government treats the press.

Public trust is the base of the triangle, and government and news are the sides. The closer government and news come to each other, the less public trust there is. When government and the news source are identical, there is no public trust at all. So there is a tension, a pressure, at each angle. History tells us that democracy can exist only within the triangle, that is, when the public perceives a space between the government and the news sources. That is why the relationship between broadcasters and government is not merely a professional issue.

We should add that we are not using *trust* in this context to mean an uncritical or even sympathetic acceptance, but rather being able to rely upon these institutions for the performance of familiar and needed services.

This inter-relationship forms the most critical and certainly the most controversial area in the world of television news, an area we will explore in this chapter. But first we would like to set a scene.

There is a Winnebago parked about a hundred feet from a small house. Cotton fields stretch out on either side. The house is hardly a house—a tiny tar-paper shack where an old woman, "Big Mama," lives with some chickens and pigs to keep her company. It is growing late in the afternoon, and David is sitting impatiently in the driver's seat, staring at the shack. He is wondering when the lighting man will come back. The lighting man is in there, setting up his equipment for the next day's shooting. The rest of the crew—soundman, cameraman, researcher—have finished. Everyone is thinking about the motel, which is almost forty miles away. They are all tired. They are looking forward to a hot shower, a drink, a steak, and the kind of horsing around that releases the tension built up during a long day in the field. Finally Morty, the lighting man, two hundred and fifty pounds of Brooklyn, returns. He climbs into the van with a gracefulness that a surprising number of very large people display. "We're ready to go," he says. "That is if we don't burn the place down." "What's the problem?" David, who is the producer, asks. "Oh, just that the ceilings in there are cardboard—probably came from boxes. These spots get

Barbara Walters, who became the first female evening news coanchor and first woman to earn one million dollars in salary per year, with Harry Reasoner.
*Source:* ABC

really hot. They might just set if off." A headline flashes through his mind: "CBS NEWS CREW INCINERATES EL-DERLY BLACK WOMAN."

That was an episode in the making of a CBS News documentary—a two-hour study of a 1970s trend: the rise of significant numbers of black families from poverty to the entry-level of the middle class. The younger generations' stories had been filmed in Kansas City and Atlanta. This part was about their parents and grandparents and their beginnings in a low-lying Mississippi cotton field, the literal origin being the eighty-year-old double amputee "Big Mama" herself.

The objective was to film an annual Thanksgiving reunion. The next day somewhere between seventy-five and one hundred family members would be there—five generations from more than a dozen states—bringing into the little shack all the fixings for the feast and all the memories of a time gone by.

That simple setup was the essence of news—taking the cameras out into the world. No definition fits every circumstance, but perhaps the major distinction of news is that the content precedes the production. Entertainment is the opposite. The job in entertainment is to bring the content into being; the job of news is to report content that is already there. The two approaches involve very different responsibilities and raise different issues.

For example, no one questions the playwright's right to invent characters, a plot, and the lines the actors will speak. The only issue in question is skill. The reporter is in a different position. His material is already out there. He has far less control over it, but because the material has its roots in the real world, the exercise of that control is far more controversial. Questions of distortion, manipulation, and falsehood inevitably arise. Everything in the process is questioned—the intent, the degree, and the methodology of control from initial story selection to final presentation. Control, then, is the first issue in news—a fact recognized by the First Amendment, which deals with exactly that.

Until recently, in most of the world, news sources were under the direct control of governments. What was reported and how it was reported were matters of government policy. This policy is ultimately self-defeating for governments. When the governments of the communist block came under pressure from their own people, for example, they found that control of untrusted news media was of no value. They discovered that credibility cannot be mandated; it must be earned. Even for a medium as powerful as television, even with sight, sound, and motion at their command, the government still had to contend with human nature. This is the angle from which American news organizations have to deal with the issue of credibility; they must earn acceptance from the public. They are privately owned, which means that they do not have the authority of the

One of the most credible news programs and the most successful weekly show in the history of television is "60 Minutes." The show's 1994 correspondents (*from left*): Morley Safer, Mike Wallace, Ed Bradley, Leslie Stahl, and Steve Croft.
*Source:* CBS News

government (or its threat of force) behind them. They are obliged to establish their own authority through their own practices. They decide what will be reported and how it will be reported, powers that are generally summed up by the term *editorial control.* A favorite pastime in America is arguing over how responsibly that control is exercised—what standards prevail, what influences these judgments, and how trustworthy is the reporting. These issues are not merely academic. It is apparent that a democracy cannot function without a free flow of reliable information. In the business itself, credibility is considered to be a news organization's chief—some would say its only—asset. In that sense, the business and the social objectives are congruent if not identical. It should be added that years of surveys indicate that news on television enjoys a very high level of public confidence.

Although they are shielded from government interference by the First Amendment, it is not true that news organizations have no relationship to the government. The government, as the main instrument of power, is almost invariably the main source of news. Historically, government has always wanted its own views, its own version of events, and its own proposals for how to deal with those events to prevail. And historically, the reporter, after reporting the government's views, has sought out and reported other views, informing the public of other facts, other proposals, and other explanations. Government reaction to this activity is often one of displeasure. This is where an understanding of the difference between the terms *fair* and *favorable* is important. When charges of unfairness are made, it is usually the case that a story is unfavorable to an interested party's position. In the case of broadcasting and government, their relationship is further compounded by the fact that it is the government that licenses broadcasters. There have been incidents in which government figures have threatened to take action against the licenses of offending television organizations. The record, thus far, indicates the threats were ineffective.

The fact that the news is financed from private sources introduces another influence. Those sources exist in a market economy. This means that the news process, no matter how carefully it is protected, cannot be entirely shielded from economic considerations. The most commonly cited fear is that news is inevitably tailored to suit the tastes of its audience rather than the judgment of the journalist. The theory is that sensationalism wins out over significance. In practice, the appetite for information in today's America is so robust that both win a place. The marketplace supports both, although perhaps for different reasons and perhaps with significantly different consequences for the provider. The networks, still by far the largest providers of news, have much more to lose by compromising standards than their newer competitors do.

Television news fills a variety of roles and has a special set of responsibilities. At the network level, it is a watchdog, keeping an eye on government and other power centers of society, as well as reporting on national and world affairs. At the local level, it is a watchdog, too, plus a community informer, a combination of sounding board and bulletin board. In both network and local versions, it is a program source, meaning it is both an expense and an income item. This is the business side of news, the underpinning that makes these roles possible. News in this system must work because it makes business sense, or it will not work at all. Let's consider this proposition in greater detail.

There are two ways in which news as it presently exists in the system could be radically changed. One is through competitive pressures that would force the traditional broadcasters, who provide the bulk of the news, to reduce sharply or even abandon their efforts. As we have said elsewhere in this book, despite forecasts to the contrary, we see no reason to expect this to happen in the near future.

The other way is through government intervention, either direct intervention in the editorial process, or indirect intervention in the business structure supporting news. Although there are certain specific ways in which the First Amendment rights of broadcasters are more limited than those of the print press, there does not seem to be any serious prospect that they will be withdrawn. But there is a long history of government intervention in the business of broadcasting, and it is not inconceivable that this could have the unintended side effect of undercutting the economic base that supports news services. For example, in 1971, the advertising of cigarettes was banned, abruptly removing one of the major categories of broadcast income. Here are some other examples:

In 1959, the Federal Communications Commission began to study television industry practices surrounding the production, ownership, and distribution of programs. It concluded that the networks dominated the process, determining "what the American people see and hear during the hours when most Americans view television." By 1970, the Commission had adopted the following rules that directly affected the networks' programming role:

1. The Prime Time Access Rule (PTAR). Prior to this rule, the networks programmed three-and-a-half hours in prime time (7:30 P.M. to 11:00 P.M.). This rule says the networks cannot provide more than three hours of prime-time programming in the top fifty markets per night. In most cities, the networks ceased to program 7:30–8:00 P.M., EST.

Since it is not practical to produce programming exclusively for the stations below this level, this rule had the effect of removing two-and-a-half hours a week from each network's program schedule. Because three networks were affected, the actual total of programming time reserved for nonnetwork sources came to one-and-a-half hours per night.

2. The Financial Interest Rule. This rule says that the networks cannot acquire any financial interest in outside productions or in the business of distributing them. Since the networks have little production capability, this effectively takes them out of the business of owning programs. In addition, the consent decrees with the Justice Department put further limits on the number of hours that can be broadcast each week.

3. The Syndication Rule. This says the networks can not sell, license, or distribute programs for off-network showing

within the United States. Since this is more or less the other half of the Financial Interest Rule, the two became known collectively as the Financial Interest and Syndication Rules.

The net effect of all this was to take the networks out of a marketplace that was worth billions of dollars. For example, programs like *M\*A\*S\*H* or *The Cosby Show* have earned hundreds of millions of dollars in off-network repeats, but the networks that paid for their development and for the right to show them (CBS and NBC, respectively) do not share in those revenues. A change like that affects the configuration of a business. In 1993, the FCC proposed substantial relaxation of the restrictions imposed on the networks by the Financial Interest and Syndication Rules. This is now scheduled to take effect in 1995.

The PTAR had another, unintended, side effect. In the 1980s serious pressure was building to lengthen the networks' evening news broadcasts from a half-hour to a full hour. However, loss of the 7:30 P.M. time period now meant that to do this, a network would have to obtain a local half-hour to match the existing network news half-hour. For many reasons, the networks' affiliates were not eager to do this, so the full-hour evening news never became a reality.

Two other issues that continue to hold Washington's attention and receive extra notice during presidential election years are the high cost of television advertising time and the equal-time provision of the Communications Act of 1934. Because of the high cost of campaigning for public office, there is a body of opinion that says that politicians should receive free TV advertising. At a breakfast meeting in the presidential election year of 1988, Gene discussed the issue with a former mayor of New York City, John Lindsay.

John Lindsay expected the breakfast to be just another meal, as business meals go: an English muffin, toast, perhaps some scrambled eggs. Big breakfasts are out in an office setting; they can be fun in the north woods, but north of Fiftieth Street, they can be a sluggish way to begin a day. But when he jokingly said he expected to have kippers, Gene accepted the challenge. He was quite surprised when Madelline, the cook, served them to him.

John Lindsay's laughing reaction to kippers for breakfast in a CBS executive dining room soon gave way to a more serious discussion of the role of television in an election year. He had recently returned from a seminar on that very topic. The participants included broadcasters, politicians, and academics. They spent three days arguing the proper use of the medium in the election process. In his words, nothing revolutionary occurred. Each group defended the position it brought with it. Any intelligent observer could have forecast that outcome.

Gene had recently attended a similar two-day event, at the Kennedy School of Government at Harvard University. That session also brought together academics, politicians, and broadcasters.

The issue has been frequently debated in the years that followed those meetings, just as it was in prior election years. No resolution has been found that is able to satisfy all participants. The debate's relevance here is that network television has a major stake in the issue.

The reason so many highly qualified people have found no simple solution to what is perceived by some as a simple problem—just give them free time—is the usual one: the problem isn't simple.

For example, to most incumbents there is no problem. Which is to say, few of them find any virtue in allowing their challengers instant parity in the medium. This is hardly surprising, but it also suggests the difficulty of getting any legislation through. The challengers hold to the opposite view. They see free television time as a leap forward in the democratic process—at least until they are elected.

Broadcasters look at this and wonder why they are being asked to subsidize political campaigns. Under most proposals, candidates could spend all they want on newspapers, billboards, matchbook covers, banners, hats, or free lunches, but not on television. And all of the purveyors of these traditional campaign accoutrements can make all of these items anybody wants to order. Once a broadcaster gives away time, it is gone forever. He cannot expand his inventory.

Also, the cost of making free time available could be significant to broadcasters. In 1980, one free-time proposal would have compelled the CBS station in New York to provide ninety-nine hours of free political advertising in prime time—almost three hours per night—during thirty-five consecutive nights preceding the election. That amounts to displacing the entire prime-time schedule for a month. Aside from a staggering revenue loss for the station, there is the question of how viewers would respond. The answer is simple: they would switch channels.

This example speaks to one of the thorniest questions in the debate: If a free-time proposal was enacted, what would the ground rules be?

Someone would have to define who qualified. All candidates? Or only those who could be defined as realistic entries? And what would the criteria be? Someone would have to decide how much time qualifiers would get. Someone would have to decide at what point in the electoral process free time would officially start, and at what point it would officially stop. Someone would have to decide at what hours the free time would run. Someone would have to decide on what channels it would be carried and how to equalize individual candidates' exposure (political programming run opposite a fishing show is one thing; opposite *60 Minutes* it is another).

Even assuming these problems could be resolved, free time for candidates is a considerable bureaucratic intrusion into our political process.

How is it justified? The answer is money. The expense of television commercials is such, the argument goes, that only the wealthy or those supported by powerful special-interest groups can now run for office. The result, it is said, is antidemocratic.

But consider these points. Television commercial time is expensive. It is expensive because advertisers value it highly. Advertisers value it highly because it is the most efficient medium available to them. That is, it costs them less through television than any other medium to reach customers with impact. So the value that is at issue is the value put upon TV by the free marketplace. A free-time proposal would simply override that. Another way to look at it is that it would penalize television for its efficiency.

A counterargument is that it is not a question of efficiency but of sheer magnitude. Television eats up so much money that it puts a run for office beyond the reach of all but the privileged, or captive, few. But this is really an argument about the cost of campaigning in America, not the cost of television. And the biggest influence on the cost of campaigning is the length of the campaign. It would make more sense to place limits on the allowable time for campaigning than to artificially control the use of one medium in a campaign. The issue received attention again during the primary campaign for the 1992 presidential election.

One of the laws governing broadcasters is Section 315 of the Communications Act of 1934. It provides that if a station licensee lets a legally qualified candidate use the station, other candidates for the same office have to be given "equal opportunities" to use the station. If one got free time, all had to get free time; if one paid, all others were entitled to the same rates. Commonly referred to as the Equal Time Provision, the rule states that, if there are, for example, six presidential candidates seeking the nomination to represent the Democratic Party, and the station provides ten free minutes to one, the station must be prepared to provide ten free minutes to the other five. Or, if it gives an hour to one, it must give an hour to all the others. This specific point came into play in 1980.

CBS News did a full-hour interview with Senator Ted Kennedy before he had formally announced his candidacy for the Democratic nomination for President. Between the filming and the scheduled air date he made some remarks that could have been—or perhaps not—interpreted as the equivalent of a formal declaration. The drama concerning the application of the Equal Time Provision was played out behind the walls of CBS corporate headquarters. What made it into something more than a daunting economic issue was an unexpected moment of revelation in the program itself. It involved David sitting in a private screening room at CBS News, viewing a "work print" of the broadcast.

The opening shot showed Ted Kennedy seated outdoors somewhere in the Hyannisport complex, facing Roger Mudd, the CBS News correspondent. Roger started off with the most obvious question: "Senator, why do you want to be President of the United States?" There was a long, painful pause. It seemed to go on, and on, and on. This was an early, rough cut, used only for executive screenings, so David thought it might still contain some technical lapse. What else could explain Kennedy's apparent bafflement at this question? But no, it was real. Slowly Kennedy fumbled his way into a confused and startlingly hesitant response. The interview had turned up political dynamite in the least expected way.

Some critics believe that Kennedy's fluffed response to this question became a major handicap in his search for the nomination, but the immediate question for CBS was whether it would ever be seen. At that point he had shown an interest in running but had not officially declared his candidacy. However, between the filming and the date at which the broadcast was to be scheduled, he had done some things that some observers felt were tantamount to a de facto declaration. If that had been the case, the documentary might not have been broadcast, since CBS would have had to provide free hours to all of those who were running, causing a calamitous dislocation of the schedule. CBS had to make that judgment. There were problems either way: not to broadcast might appear to be suppression of important information; broadcasting meant significant dislocation in the schedule.

This occurred almost a year before the actual election. The point is that what ought to be a news judgment became a quasilegal judgment. Broadcasters become cautious in these circumstances. It is simpler not to do this kind of program at all, and as a result, election-year coverage is less aggressive than it would otherwise be. It is worth adding that the FCC itself has recommended eliminating Section 315, calling it "an unnecessary and detrimental regulatory mechanism," which "disserves the public interest."

As a practical matter, television stations that need to make a profit to operate successfully for the benefit of employees, shareholders, and the general public interest cannot afford to provide free time under the current laws.

### Standards and News

Credibility grows incrementally. We invent our belief in individuals or institutions because of their behavior over time, because we learn what to expect from them. It can also be lost incrementally, through seepage. That is why there is a dividing line at CBS between news and entertainment, between being a journalist and being an actor. The question of consistency is involved. Here again we need to set a scene.

It was the fiftieth anniversary of CBS, and a week of specials had been planned to celebrate it. Alexander Cohen, a distinguished Broadway producer and probably the most capable man for this sort of assignment, was in charge. Early on Gene was on his way to the west coast, and he stopped at a

Frank Stanton frequently testified before Congress on behalf of the broadcasting industry, while president of CBS.
*Source:* CBS Inc.

meeting of CBS' Affiliate Advisory Board in Phoenix. While he was there, Oscar Katz, the CBS programming executive assigned to the project, took him aside and told him in worried tones that the president of CBS News had said that no newspeople would be allowed to take part in the event. Oscar could not see how we could celebrate fifty years of CBS without the likes of Cronkite, Collingwood, Reasoner, Bradley, Wallace, Edwards, Hottelet, Kuralt, Rather, and the rest. These were some of the most famous names ever associated with the company, and—unlike the entertainment stars—they were our own employees.

There was a reason for this decision. CBS had long had a rule that CBS News correspondents could not appear on entertainment programs. CBS wanted to maintain a strict separation between the two functions. It was felt that a reporter appearing in a fictional setting risked losing credibility as a serious journalist. Gene agreed with that rule but also felt an exception could be made for a one-time-only event that was in the nature of a history itself—a history these people had helped to make—and where they would appear only as themselves.

But that wasn't Oscar's only problem. The network had not been able to get Red Skelton to agree to appear. That would leave a gaping hole in the CBS tapestry. Oscar said that every time they called Red, he would answer with one word—"demographics"—and hang up. Skelton was referring to the reason given for the cancellation of his show some eight years earlier. Gene told Oscar he would try to solve both problems.

As it happens, an acceptable arrangement for the newspeople to appear was worked out, and Red Skelton did finally agree to appear—after Gene pointed out that he would be the only star who had appeared in the historic twenty-fifth anniversary photo at MGM and in the CBS fiftieth.

There were seven nights of shows, but in only one of them, more than one hundred stars associated with CBS, past and present, were to appear. Gene went to CBS Television City in Hollywood on the day of that taping. The scene in the big studio was extraordinary and probably will never be equaled again. There were dozens of world-famous people lining up at a score of makeup stations as though they were buying train tickets. Red Skelton was on one of the lines. He had had a rousing welcome from the technicians and stagehands when he arrived back at the studio where he had done his show for so many years. He was glowing. Gene went over to thank him for coming. As they were talking, Skelton looked at the line across from his, gasped, pointed, and said, "Look! that's Eric Sevareid! Imagine that! This must be an important event!"

What Skelton had unwittingly done was demonstrate the effectiveness of the news-entertainment separation policy that had been suspended for this occasion. To Red Skelton, Eric Sevareid was a celebrity of another sort, a great figure in a world apart from his. That is exactly what CBS wished its audiences to recognize. Journalism was one thing; entertainment was another. It is a policy that has slowly eroded over recent years, as newspeople have made periodic appearances on entertainment programs dealing with fictitious stories and characters, to what we think is the detriment of both parties.

The CBS News standards evolved over time out of experiences gained in the field. They were eventually formalized as written rules because it was believed that the guidance they provided needed to be transmitted throughout the entire news-gathering organization for the long-term benefit of the organization itself and for the benefit of the viewing public. CBS was not so naive as to believe that an activity as unpredictable and spontaneous as news coverage could be pursued with a rule book in hand, but it remained that everybody in the organization needed to know what was acceptable and what was not. And—perhaps equally important—everybody needed to understand the frame of mind the standards represented. As standards erode, quality suffers.

It was commitment to the importance of standards that resulted in a detailed internal investigation of a CBS documentary, "The Uncounted Enemy," and eventually led to an extended trial and what is probably the most exhaustive investigation of a news program ever undertaken. After *TV Guide* alleged that the program, as produced, violated specific CBS News standards, Gene ordered an investigation to determine the truth. This was a necessary step if the standards were to mean anything and if CBS News' reputation for honesty, integrity, and fairness were to remain intact. Credibility is the lifeblood of a news organization. A respect for standards, therefore, requires answers to accusations that challenge credibility. The CBS investigation did uncover some violations of policy, but they did not compromise the integrity of the documentary's premise. Ironically, the report revealed that had all of the proper procedures been followed during the production, it would have resulted in a stronger documentary.

The NBC network had problems with a documentary it produced regarding certain trucks built by General Motors. An investigation uncovered the fact that the producer enhanced the explosion of a truck's gas tank and, in so doing, misled the public. GM sued NBC. Even thogh a settlement was reached, the network's image was tarnished.

Again, if quality is important, standards need to exist. If quality is not important, standards are not necessary. But when standards are abandoned, only the competition benefits.

Edward R. Murrow spoke to a troublesome aspect of this issue—the role of the profit motive—in an address to the Radio and Television News Directors Association in Chicago in 1958: "There is no suggestion here that networks or individual stations would operate as philanthropies. But I can find nothing in the Bill of Rights or the Communication Act which says that they must increase their net profits each year lest the Republic collapse."

Murrow was discussing the public service responsibilites of broadcasters. He characterized those responsibilities as a choice between more profit and less profit, but not no profit. It is clear which side he was on. This position was extremely popular with news directors, who comprised the audience in the hall at the time. News directors did not have profit responsibilities. It was not so popular with those who did, including the top management of CBS, who felt Murrow had no business getting into this area in the first place and that he was deliberately setting them up. If they were seen as having to choose between more profit and more public service, then only one path was open. So, even in the simpler and still growing marketplace of 1958, there was real tension between public service requirements and the demands of business. The conflict is far more severe today in a more competitive marketplace. Yet, ironically, it may be that public service is more important to the survival of broadcasters now than ever. Before we discuss why, a little history is in order.

In 1980, Ronald Reagan appointed Mark Fowler chairman of the Federal Communications Commission, with a mandate to preside over a sweeping program of deregulation. Part of this was known as "cleaning out the underbrush"— getting rid of a host of relatively obscure regulations that had accumulated over the years and were considered to be no longer appropriate. One of the items that went—without any particular fanfare—was the so-called Trafficking Rule. This was a requirement that a broadcast license be held for a minimum of three years. The intent of this rule was to discourage speculation in licenses. It was believed that venture capital would not support the large investments required to buy television stations if the money was tied up for less than three years. The other side of this was the belief that under these circumstances, the only investors who would come forward were those genuinely interested in operating stations for the long haul and that these people would be mindful of their obligations regarding "the public interests, convenience and necessity." So there had been a subtle but real connection between the Trafficking Rule and public service programming.

The removal of the rule undercut this connection by effectively transforming television licenses into commodities, that is, properties that could be traded over the short term. The result was an overnight infusion of venture capital into the industry. Between 1983 and 1986, 370 stations with a combined value of $10 billion changed hands—more stations and some five times as much money as in the previous ten years. Operating stations was no longer the only way—and perhaps not even the best way—to make a profit from them.

However, by 1987 the entire industry was caught in the recession. The bull market for stations dried up. The easy turnover anticipated by many new owners did not materialize. In its place was a heavy interest payment requirement, putting even more pressure on the bottom line. In these circumstances, public service programming becomes a ready cost-cutting target, even for the more substantial operators.

None of this appears at first sight to be a scenario for reviving support for the concept of serving "the public interest, convenience and necessity." Yet that is the case we will argue, that what began as legislation has now become logical as well.

The reasoning behind this position is very simple. The more crowded a marketplace becomes, the more critical identity becomes. The networks have a unique position as principal managers of the production-distribution-funding cycle. They also have, through their own resources and those of their affiliates, a unique public service capacity—three separate worldwide news gathering organizations backed up by some six hundred local news bureaus. This is an incredibly complex, costly, and irreplaceable capital base that has no equal in the world. It was built incrementally over a seventy-year period and cannot be duplicated. Through it broadcasters can connect the public with those aspects of our collective life that are summed up in the term "public interest." No other electronic medium can do this.

No newer source has this capacity—not cable, not high-powered satellites, not HDTV (high-definition television), not smarter computers, not the entry of the telephone companies into the field. The marketplace distinction open to the traditional broadcaster is, ironically, the oldest one in the game: filling a need better than anyone else. For networks and their affiliates this would mean more serious news and public affairs programming when the trend has been toward less. This is not an easy choice. The temptation is to do this only when the costs are low, as they are in the case of a number of the current prime-time news hours. The criterion should not be costs alone, but whether a valuable service is being added. The benefits have to be measured in broad terms. Nonetheless, benefits there are. Over the years, the strongest station in the market is likely to be the one with the strongest record of community service. According to a National Association of Broadcasters (NAB) study of network affiliates' cash flows in 1991, there was a positive relationship between average cash flow and news expenditures for affiliates in the top twenty-five markets. Also, expenditures on news showed no significant drop from the prior year, despite a difficult business environment—a sign that broadcasters continue to recognize the value of this franchise.

The young Fox Network, successful as it is, has recognized what its older colleagues have always known: a serious news and public affairs effort is essential to its business. And, while this book has been critical in other places of the under-investment in product that has characterized much of the cable industry, it cannot be denied that CNN is an example of what a unique, well-managed, and, for that matter, stylistically conservative news and public affairs service can do for the reputation of its supplier—and this is with an audience one-tenth the size of any one of the networks' evening news broadcasts.

Washington continues to be among television's severest critics. In the next chapter we will revisit, and reconsider, one of the most famous critical attacks ever made on the medium by a government figure.

# Chapter 5

## Television and Its Critics

The most prestigious gathering in television is the annual convention of the National Association of Broadcasters. Everybody who is anybody goes—the station owners, the general managers, the program directors, the news directors, the sales managers, the top executives of the networks, the program producers, the hardware makers, the top advertising people, the station representative organizations, the trade groups, the regulators, the lawyers for everybody, the consultants for everybody, the press, and everyone who counts from Washington, New York, and Los Angeles, the three power centers of the industry, and almost every place in between.

Having all this power in one place does not necessarily mean that anything interesting happens, but the 1961 convention did have a particular electricity about it. In 1958, the quiz show scandal had rocked the industry. It had been revealed over the course of a nine-month grand jury probe and sensational public hearings by a subcommittee of the U.S. House of Representatives that the most popular shows on television— big money quizzes, such as *The $64,000 Question, The $64,000*

*Challenge,* and *Twenty-One*—were frauds. Contestants who seemed to be answering incredibly difficult questions spontaneously had been given the answers beforehand. The national shock wave that resulted from this revelation was compounded by the fact that dozens of the people involved—the contestants, the shows' producers, and television executives—repeatedly lied to the investigators and the grand jury about their roles when the first inklings of impropriety came out. Perhaps the supreme irony was that at the time there was nothing illegal about rigging a quiz show. It was another legal point that led to criminal charges. It had to do with the difference between lying and perjury. It is not perjury to lie to the police or the District Attorney, but it is perjury to lie to a grand jury because the witnesses are under oath. And many of those involved did lie, despite clear warnings about the consequences. As one of the chief investigators put it, it was "a story of extortion, of larceny, of obstruction of justice, of perjury, of lying so pervasive that it was woven into the fabric of American life."*

Although the big stories had already broken when the convention began, the investigations were still under way. But legal technicalities were not the issue as far as the public was concerned. For them it was very simple: they had been had by the networks. Although the networks—chiefly NBC and CBS—responded by canceling the quiz shows and introducing full-hour documentaries in prime time in a conspicuous public service effort, the shadow cast by this sordid episode remained. There might be good shows and bad shows, silly shows and fascinating shows, but deliberate deception was intolerable. Everyone knew that. What gave the scandal its notoriety was a growing sense of television's power. A few months earlier the nation had seen the Great Debates, as candidates Kennedy and Nixon faced each other before the television cameras. Many

---

*For a full and fascinating account of this episode, see *Prime Time and Misdemeanors* by Joseph Stone and Tim Yohn.

His "vast wasteland" speech in 1961 made Newton Minow one of the most notable of FCC chairmen.
*Source:* CBS Inc.

believed that those debates had been a deciding factor in the outcome of the election.

It was in this climate that the most powerful single person in broadcasting, Newton Minow, the man John F. Kennedy had just appointed chairman of the Federal Communications Commission, was scheduled to make his first address before the most powerful assemblage of broadcasters in the world. That speech entered history, not so much for its substance, which was a not unfamiliar combination of reprimands and entreaties, but because of a single phrase. The new chairman told the broadcasters that what they had created, what they presided over and were making fortunes from, was nothing more than a "vast wasteland," a kind of cultural desert in which they had neglected their service to the public in pursuit of profits and popularity—what he called the "Dictatorship of Numbers."

A general tone of rebuke was standard regulator-to-regulatees talk. After all, broadcasters held licenses from the government that required them to serve "the public interest, convenience and necessity." It was Minow's job to see that they

did. Minow was hardly the first FCC chairman to find them
wanting. But defining their medium as a "vast wasteland"
stretched their shortcomings well beyond the usual bound-
aries. It suggested more than failure; it suggested guilt for the
willful despoilation of a natural resource; a resource that be-
longed to the people. There was desolation abroad in TV land,
and there was no doubt somebody was to blame. The broadcasters.

If what they were doing wasn't what they ought to be doing,
what was? Minow told them: "You must help prepare a generation for great decisions. You must help a great nation fulfill its
future." The speech thus combined a devastating indictment
with a call to glory. For those who listened carefully, it could be
noted that both depended upon the same assessment of the
inherent power of television. Without that, neither the charge
of failure nor the promise of greatness was meaningful.

Being called the proprietors of a "vast wasteland" would
have been disturbing coming from anyone, but in this case the
speaker was not anyone. He was the leader of the organization
that licensed stations, the one authority who could put a broadcaster out of business overnight. By addressing the question of
operating in the public interest, Minow had placed himself
squarely in the area of license renewals—the realm of a broadcaster's worst nightmares. In case anyone missed the point, he
hit it with a sledgehammer: "There is nothing permanent or
sacred about a broadcast license," he reminded them.

As it happened, no licenses were canceled, but it is likely
that at least a number of licensees took a closer look at their
statutory obligations after hearing Minow. This was unquestionably the most memorable speech ever delivered at the convention and one of the few that transcended its setting. That
centerpiece image—the "vast wasteland"—struck a chord with
critics. It became a cultural byword, the media equivalent of
terms like *Cold War* and *Iron Curtain*. As recently as December
1992, it showed up in the headline of a Sunday *New York Times*

piece by critic John O'Connor. "Still Trapped in Vast Wasteland" was the title. Part of O'Connor's distress with the networks was based on his notion of their failure to realize the
benefits of a new freedom, since they had been "released from
regulatory handcuffs during the Reagan-Bush era." But no
such thing had happened. It was cable that had been deregulated. No network deregulation had occurred at that point, yet
here was a veteran observer for a major newspaper who seemed
unaware of it.

Because it embodies a particular view of television, and
because that view leads to the question of how we actually use
television, the judgment implied by the "vast wasteland" is
worth serious examination. The question to be put is not
whether an eager new regulator was leveling unfair criticisms,
but whether his assessment of the medium was reasonable. For
it is that—the question of what television can and cannot do—
that conditions all of our expectations about it.

Minow himself revisited that speech in the fall of 1991.
Recalling his own remarks thirty years later, he pointed out
that the two words he had hoped to be remembered for were
not "vast wasteland," but "public service," the area in which
he believed then, and believes now, the medium has not measured up. In the new speech (titled "How Vast the Wasteland
Now?") he asked the following question: "Which of the following is the most important educational institution in America:
(a) Harvard, (b) Yale, (c) Columbia, (d) the University of
California, or (e) none of the above. His answer was (e). "The
most important educational institution in America is television."

Minow could point to support for this position from no less
a source than America's premiere journalist, E. B. White.
White had once written: "We shall stand or fall by television . . . of that I am sure. . . . I believe television is going
to be the test of the modern world."

Minow and White share the view that television is an overriding cultural force, a medium capable of instructing an entire society, for better or (as in Minow's wasteland) for worse. That assessment is what leads to the indictments. And they are legion. They are echoed in speeches, papers, articles, books, and commentaries (including those of many distinguished television personages) from almost every authoritative source we have—government, academia, religion, science, industry, and the arts. The surprising thing about this criticism is not its existence, but the fact that its premises are so rarely examined. For instance, it might be asked what Minow means when he calls television "the most important educational institution in America." His answer was that "more people learn more each hour, each day, each year, each lifetime from television than from any other source." But what he is talking about is exposure, not learning as it is offered in our educational institutions. He equates exposure to a television screen with exposure to the entire apparatus of a genuine educational institution—a teacher, a curriculum, texts, and exams, all of which are accompanied by conditions for acceptance, attendance, and matriculation. Television has none of these characteristics. It is not in any commonly accepted usage of the term an educational institution at all. It is a source of information and entertainment—a far different thing.

Further, educational institutions have punitive powers; those of the earliest stages also have, literally, police powers, such as truancy laws. This is not by accident. It has been found that education, defined as the transmission of prescribed bodies of information, requires it to be effective. Students need to be enclosed in special protected spaces called classrooms. To get them to respond, threats as well as rewards are used. Tests are necessary; failure occurs. An entire profession exists to enforce these measures. Huge sums are expended on the physical apparatus, from buildings to blackboards, necessary to this system. Neither television nor any other medium has any of these characteristics. Television is no more an educational institution than books, movies, plays, magazines, or newspapers are. All of them can inform and can be used in an educational process, but education, as in an educational institution, is not, nor could it be, their first purpose.

Minow knew all this. He also knew that he needed to get the broadcasters' attention, and he did. He did not retract anything when he returned to the scene thirty years later, because his thinking about the medium had not changed. As far as he was concerned, television's educational potential was not being realized then, nor is it now. The problem is whether his definition is reasonable.

E. B. White is a different case. He was not a newly appointed regulator trying to make an impression. He was a distinguished journalist noted for the sanity and clarity of his style. He had no stake in either promoting or belittling television. It should be added, however, that he was speaking before there was a record to examine. He had seen only a very early experimental version of the new medium. In those circumstances, perhaps it is all the more surprising that he should go so far as to suggest that television is to be the test of the modern world. This is not Minow phrase-making for a headline; this is a serious writer, on a subject he knows—communications. What can White have meant? His explanation is not very helpful: "In this new opportunity to see beyond a subject, beyond the range of our vision, we shall discover either a new and unbearable disturbance to the general peace, or a saving radiance in the sky." The most common criticism of television is that people spend too much time with it. That seems the very opposite of an unbearable disturbance to the general peace. At the other extreme, what could White have envisioned as a saving radiance in the sky? What pictures, what words, what in art or science could provide what sounds like salvation?

Minow's positioning of television as our leading educational institution and White's even loftier view of it as the testing ground of the modern world as well as similar views held by flocks of critics before and after them, seem to rest on two shared beliefs. One is very old—the idea that there is such a thing as a "higher" culture, and that it is good for you. The other is newer—faith in the near magical powers of new technologies.

Put together, these two beliefs led to another—that in television was to be found the means of spreading the higher culture far and wide. It would, at last, reach the masses. Here is how Minow put it in the original wasteland speech: "The power of instantaneous sight and sound is without precedent in mankind's history. . . . It has limitless capabilities for good—or for evil." But it really was not just the power of instantaneous sight and sound that fascinated. If you took away sports, there wasn't much instantaneous sight and sound on the air, and for fifty years, movies had had the rest—sight, sound, and motion—in a bigger and better version. The kicker with television was the audience. It was the thought of those millions of viewers out there every night planted in front of all those screens that was irresistible.

On that point there was no argument. By the time Minow made his speech, television was being watched for more than forty hours a week in American homes. Sitting there day in and day out was the largest and most faithful audience the world had ever known. What Minow, White, and so many others wanted was to treat this audience as a kind of monumental class. They wanted them instructed. There was only one problem. That audience was not there to watch what Minow or any other theorist wanted them to watch. It was there for what it liked best—Milton Berle and Jackie Gleason and Lucy and *Bonanza* and *Gunsmoke*. In the system as it actually was, the "best" of anything was going to have to compete with the best jokes and the best action, and there was no doubt which would win. Minow knew this. This is what he meant by the Dictatorship of Numbers—the preference for the popular. His position was that it was up to the broadcasters to do something about this, to lift the audience to the higher culture. The unstated precondition of his vision of the broadcasters' public service obligation was to find a way to keep the audience, without giving them what they wanted. To do this was simply to put his goals ahead of the viewers'. This is a position that reappears again and again in the literature on television. A recent example is to be found in a book called *The Good Society*.

The premise of *The Good Society* is that we live in and through institutions—family, school, community, corporation, church, state, and nation—and that only by taking responsibility for those institutions can we take responsibility for ourselves and improve our lives.

What we would like to discuss here is how the authors position television in their hierarchy of cultural values. Here is a passage from the book's conclusion:

> Unfortunately, many of the distractions we hope will "deaden the pain"—alcohol; restless channel-flipping TV watching; compulsive promiscuity—do not really help, for such distractions too are forms of alienated attention that leave us mildly, or sometimes severely, depressed. We have not exercised the potentialities of our selves and our relationships, and so we have not reaffirmed ourselves in the larger contexts that give our lives meaning. If, after a stressful day, we can turn our attention to something that is mildly demanding, but inherently meaningful—reading a good book, repairing the car, talking to someone we love, or even cooking the family meal—we are more apt to find that we are "relaxed."

Television viewing is likened to alcoholism and licentiousness. The other medium mentioned, books, joins a list of benign domestic activities. One could reverse this and suggest that flipping restlessly through the pages of books is not necessarily rewarding (though presumably not as bad as boozing and whoring), and that viewing a "good" television program might be worthwhile. There is more than an echo of the famous "vast wasteland" speech here. Minow's position differed in that television was presented as a wasted opportunity, not as a kind of evil in and of itself. In *The Good Society,* the prescription is that we ought to cut down on television and get back to books if we want to improve not just ourselves, but the whole society. Yet, undergirding both positions is the same view of society and the position of culture within it. There is a high and a low end to culture; one is good for you, and the other is not. Books are connected to the high end, and television to the low end. One end makes for not only a better-educated person, but a better person as well. The more of these people we have, the better our society will be. The fact that no evidence is offered in support of this conclusion is not surprising, since it is hard to come by. There is nothing that tells us that heavy readers of books, even the very "best" books, are better citizens than people who rarely turn a page, or that the society would greatly benefit if every television set were to go dark in order that more books could be read. Indeed, at least one of the more pernicious social dislocations of our time—the Savings and Loan disaster—seems to have been largely the product of very highly educated people. Yet, so ingrained is this faith in the inherent superiority of the printed page that television can be reproached simply as a distraction from books.

A not dissimilar view is held by James Billington, the current Librarian of Congress. Here is what he had to say in an article in the *Los Angeles Times* (11/15/92):

> I think it's important that libraries do the right thing. They could, as some have already done, become video stores and rent out things for people to take home and watch on their television sets. Well, I think that's a betrayal of the library. American Memory is based on audiovisual sources. But this is the crucial difference: It involves the active mind rather than the passive motions. In order to use it, you're going to generate questions that can only be answered by books that surround the material.

It's a supplement that uses new technology to reinforce old values. The appeal, as I said, is to the active mind, and that's the knowledge base of democracy.

To the Librarian of Congress, books represent the "active mind" and television is "passive motions." Books form the "knowledge base of democracy," presumably because they predate television and were around at the founding of the nation. Why this continues to be true is not made clear. This declaration might come as a surprise to the millions of Americans who followed the election year and election night on television and in the three years before that witnessed many of the historic changes in Eastern Europe by the same means.

It is certainly true that people interact differently with a printed page than with a television screen, but this in itself does not support the conclusion that one is "active," and one is "passive." Whatever cognitive distinctions may lie here, this is a simplistic position, and its kinship with the Minow and White views as well as with the position taken in *The Good Society* is obvious.

What is disturbing about all of this is its elitist tone. On what grounds does anyone have the right to say that reading something is inherently superior to watching *Oprah?* Where is it written that repairing the car will prove both relaxing and rewarding after a tough day's work, whereas watching *Murphy Brown* is merely depressing, if not downright irresponsible? On what grounds are these judgments based?

It is hard to avoid the conclusion that the justification resides in the superior wisdom of the authors. In this they are by no means alone. Here is how Leo Bogart—an internationally known public opinion specialist and former advertising executive—put it in *The American Media System and its Commercial Culture,* a recent publication fo the Gannett Foundation Media Center:

Media content has been driven primarily by the need to maximize audiences for sale rather than by the desire to communicate the truth about our world or express deep thoughts and feelings.

Left to its own devices, the public persistently drifts toward amusement rather than enlightenment, avoiding confrontation with the pressing, perhaps overwhelming problems that confront the nation and the world.

Society has a stake in maintaining standards, in upholding traditions and in raising the level of taste.

Bogart is more candid than most when he allows that confrontation is not what the viewer is looking for. He is on less solid ground when he suggests that "deep thoughts and feelings" are avoided as well, since it is inevitably his own definition of what these may be that controls his statement. What the viewer considers to be deep thoughts and feelings may be an entirely different matter.

Here we come back to the elitist core of whites, and Minow's, line of argument. What it comes down to is that programmers should present certain fare, and viewers ought to watch it, like it or not, because "society has a stake in standards."

If the stake is simply in conveying information about what is going on in the world, then the argument is valid, since this is necessary to a democracy. But what television viewer over the last forty years could have been unaware of the major issues and confrontations of our time? How would it be possible not to have seen the unfolding of the Cold War, the civil rights movement, the women's movement, the actions in Vietnam, Afghanistan, Kuwait, Somalia, and Bosnia, the national elections, the ups and downs of the economy, the great judicial decisions, the toll of crime and violence and poverty, the S&L failure, let alone the countless events and issues in city after city across the country treated on local news? The answer would probably be that these things were treated superficially, that their full depth and meaning was not explored, or at least not often enough. That is a matter of judgment, which shifts the argument to a question of degree. The other half of the issue is the entertainment side of things. Bogart's charge here amounts to the sin of escapism:

> Television drama is remote indeed from Aristotle's notions of arousal and catharsis; it teaches no significant moral lessons in the tradition of the Greek theater. It does however, teach a large number of minor moral lessons—often in contradiction to the standards of conduct to which society pays lip service—simply by virtue of its constant reiteration of the same formulaic characterizations and dilemmas. By constantly diverting us from the unpleasant realities of the human condition, it restrains us from dealing with them too closely at the same time that it protects us from feeling their full force.

This is a complex accusation, in which television appears as both sedator and arouser, performing both functions unacceptably. It is interesting to note that "teaching" is used here in the same institutionalized sense in which Minow used it. It is always an accusatory term with respect to television, which is simultaneously a failed and an all-too effective pedagogue. Not mentioned is what this suggests about the audience, which in Bogart's view turns its back on deep thoughts and feelings but absorbs like a sponge nasty "minor moral lessons."

The Dictatorship of Numbers in the minds of the critics has a least-common-denominator effect, in which the medium's need for mass audiences drives out better material. The viewer, however, lives inside another Dictatorship of Numbers—the numbers on a clock. Viewing decisions are allotments of time. So are programming decisions. That limited commodity limits everyone; the programmer cannot expand a story by adding pages to it; nobody—not even a VCR—can fit more than 180 minutes between 8:00 and 11:00 P.M. If there is a Dictatorship of Numbers, it is the consequence of what most viewers decide to do with this ultimate resource—time—over which they exercise the ultimate control.


## Considerations and Consequences

There would be no great problem if the persistently overblown expectations that have been assigned to television were nothing but that—opinions in a grand national debate. But they have often led to very specific actions, both governmental and business, with serious consequences. Behind the regulatory restrictions of the 1970s was a feeling that the networks had become an unelected second government dictating a new culture for the entire society, which amounted to a governmental endorsement of the Minow-White-Bogart views on the medium's power. Washington resented the nightly news broadcasts, which spoke to the populace more frequently, and quite possibly more persuasively, than the government. And officials who might otherwise hestitate to act against a branch of the free press had the comforting sense that they were far from the only members of the establishment who were disturbed. Many educators believed television was undermining, if not actually replacing, the classroom. In a speech to the graduates of the University of Southern California's Graduate School of Education, Dean Goodlad said that in television he had discovered the long sought-for "common classroom" of America, but he deplored its "curriculum," echoing Minow's view of television as our leading educational institution. Many moralists believed television was an insidious pulpit, preaching a hedonistic lifestyle. There is an old maxim in psychology: attitude precedes action. The attitude that television was a vast wasteland was the bedrock on which actions affecting the entire industry rested. Meanwhile, television had become the most popular medium in history. Given these assaults, it was natural for the industry to ask "what do the users think?"

## What Viewers Think about Television

CBS conducted a series of studies in this area, starting with "The People Look at Television," in 1960. The National Association of Broadcasters also conducted a study, in 1983. Studies of an industry funded by one of its own members are always suspect. The safeguard here is pure self-interest. What CBS and the NAB were looking for was information from their own customers, the viewers. It was obviously important to get it straight, since television depends entirely on public support for its existence.

We will deal here with how viewers feel about the medium, not how they feel about the programs they watch. Perhaps the best assurance of the reliability of these studies is that they yielded results that were not very reassuring to the industry. For example, what does a businessperson do with the news that his customers are using his product more but enjoying it less? Yet that is what the 1983 National Association of Broadcasters study reported. There was a good deal of controversy about this study, but a 1980 CBS study had found something similar. Summarizing "broad trends" over the past twenty years, the CBS study noted three major developments: (1) "the American public appears to have less regard for television as a medium than it did"; (2) "it uses television more, especially to keep informed"; and (3) "it enjoys it more, though it doesn't think it should."

Here is a puzzling mixture. Respect and usage seem to go in opposite directions, like a statistical affirmation of the old saw that familiarity breeds contempt. The NAB study finds people saying television is less important in their lives and less entertaining. The CBS study finds that although people have less regard for the medium, they are enjoying it more. But, it adds, the public "doesn't think it should." So both studies find unease in the viewers' relationship to the medium. Even though they are using it more, or perhaps because they are, a shadow of guilt hovers over their viewing habit. This suggests that these studies may be telling us as much about human nature as they are about television. Certainly they are telling us something about television's standing in the society. After generations of daily use, television continues to struggle for a respectable position in our value system. Why should this be? There is probably no simple answer, but insights can be gained from considering some of the factors that contribute to our value system. For instance:

**The Puritan work ethic.** It's been declared dead many times, but most observers believe it is still a powerful force among us. Television viewing brings to this ideal of effort as virtue the handicap of being effortless. It's too easy to be good for you.

**The print tradition.** Reading and writing are acquired skills, and rightly valued as such. They are still the entry points into virtually any advance in the social system. The written word carries with it thousands of years of endorsement as the true source of our culture. Sacred writings are central to our religions. The school book is the symbol of education. Written laws are the basis of our system of government. Contracts, agreements, and pronouncements become official when they are put on paper. There is a powerful sanction here. Not only has television no such sanction, but it is often characterized as the enemy of the written word. Since the medium itself is no more that than are other forms of communication that do not require literacy to be understood, such as theater, music, or movies, this view tends to be justified on a "time displacement" theory—television takes up time that should be spent with print. It is suggested that people who cannot read or write, or who do so inadequately, would improve these skills if they spent more of the time that they now spend with television working on their literacy skills. Since they already have that option, how this can be done, short of forcefully depriving them of television, is not clear.

**Elitism.** Scarcity is central to the value system. In their famous journey to the Hebrides, Samuel Johnson, perhaps the greatest coiner of epigrams the English language has ever known, says to Boswell: "Why, sir a pebble in the road is of more use than a diamond on a lady's finger, but it is not valued as such." A good deal of what we value has its roots in limited access. Things are valued because there are not many of them—they are "rare." Certain experiences are valued because they are not open to everyone. But television is the most universal medium ever to exist. It represents the exact opposite of exclusivity—the condition so important to many value judgments.

**The displacement effect.** It is not unusual for parents and teachers to feel that television has usurped part of their role. Not surprisingly, they experience both envy and guilt about this. The result is that their perception of their own use of the medium is affected by their perception of the role of the medium in other aspects of their lives. This ends in a bifocal view of television—and that is what we are dealing with here.

What is the bifocal view of television? It is the fact that television, more than any other medium we have ever had, is experienced in two ways—both as a presence in the society and as a personal encounter. These two visions of television live side by side within the individual. Let's go back to the CBS-funded study mentioned earlier. Its overview consisted of these three parts: (1) "the American public appears to have less regard for television as a medium than it did"; (2) "it uses television more, especially to keep informed"; and (3) "it enjoys it more, though it doesn't think it should."

Less regard runs alongside more use, and more use includes both more information and more enjoyment. Yet it all seems to be topped off by guilt. Strange! But perhaps not so strange at that. The same study also tracked actual enjoyment of programs watched by those who watched them. On this basis, it found that compared to earlier years "more people were enjoying more of the programs they watched." In other words, there is no ambiguity when it comes to the enjoyment of programs actually watched. The odd coupling—using it more but enjoying it less—appears when people talk about television in general, not the programs they actually watch. Part of this may be due to the cultural and social forces mentioned earlier, but there seems to be another aspect as well. This is a kind of "double vision" that comes from the increasing public perception of television as an institution, not unlike schools or government, with a presence outside their own use of it.

Some of this is the result of television's pervasiveness in our everyday lives. It is a common topic of conversation for most people, whatever their viewing habits may be. In the last decade or so, this wider awareness of television has been reinforced by the enormous increase in commentary on television. Consider the major newspapers. Once their only regular coverage of television was one television critc, who reviewed programs and wrote about the stars. Now, many newspapers have three or four (as in the case of the *New York Times*) byline reporters on the beat. What were once obscure "trade" items can now be front-page stories: complex accounts of ratings; network profit analyses; and virtually any "social impact" item—the National Institute for Mental Health report; the National Association of Broadcasters study; the Television Audience Assessment study. The public today reads about the medium as often as it reads about the programs. The medium itself is an increasingly important contributor to this process. It is a rare talk show that does not include someone talking about television. All three network morning news shows have entertainment editors, who regularly deal with television, as do many local news shows.

Television is also now an important part of higher education. It is estimated that there are more than sixty-five thousand communications majors on our college campuses. Television is likely to be at or near the center of most of their studies. Thousands of articles, papers, and theses are published each year on television (the vast majority of them highly critical). An entire generation is being exposed to a highly formalized, structured view of the medium, quite beyond their personal experience of it. The attention paid to television as a medium by other media, by television itself, and through other institutions has a reinforcement factor unlike that of almost any other subject. The same people who use the medium also hear or read about it from somebody else every day of their lives. We take this second-level awareness of television for granted, yet we don't expect to find it where other media are concerned. Few theatergoers are likely to venture an opinion on the quality of the entire legitimate theater, even if they do see a fair number of shows, and they would probably be dumbfounded if they were asked to assess the value of going to the theater. Book readers do not see reading as something that exists apart from the printed page. There is nobody researching whether reading itself is thought to be more, or less, enjoyable, than it used to be.

For all these reasons, it should not come as a surprise that there may be a discrepancy between people's opinions about television and their own use of it. There is a discrepancy here because there is a discrepancy in their experience. Some of their views are based on what they watch, and some are based on an awareness of a larger entity called "the medium," concerning which they have certain proprietary feelings. And when it comes to putting an opinion on record, yet another phenomenon becomes involved—what the social scientists call the "socially desirable response." There is a classic illustration of this. For years, if New Yorkers were asked what newspaper they read, they would give the *New York Times* a higher circulation than the *Daily News*—the reverse of reality. This was because people thought that the question reflected on them. They responded according to what value system they would like to be identified with, not according to what their reading habits actually were.

To put it another way, if people were asked how much reading they do, how many would be concerned at seeming to read too much? Indeed, how many people take pride in declaring they never read books or newspapers? The point is that they do not feel it necessary, or desirable, to declare their superiority to an entire medium. They may well specify which kinds of books and which newspapers they never read, but they are not likely to write off the entire genre as beneath them, as many do where television is concerned. This is where the heavy cultural sanctions that surround television come into play: the ease of television viewing, which sets up an association between viewing and "idle time"; the tie between learning and the printed word, from which television is excluded; the nonelitist nature of televison (nothing is more available and viewing is not an acquired skill); television resented as a usurper of parents' and teachers' roles. All of these factors push viewing and guilt closer and closer together, or at least place viewing under a cloud of illegitimacy. Under such pressures, it would be surprising to find a majority saying that they were using television more and enjoying it more—and were comfortable about that.

History tells us that a medium works its way up the value scale of a society very slowly. In his preface to "Lyrical Ballads," Wordsworth said that he was publishing his poems in the hopes of stemming some of the moral decay of his times, which was being brought on by the appearance of a lower class of literature designed for what he called "the increasing accumulation of men in cities"—that is, what we would now call mass audiences. Even then, there was something suspect about a populist medium.

## The Effect of Television on the Individual

Lurking behind both the critics' attacks and the viewers' unease is a suspicion that television not only has profound effects on viewers, but, in a sense, overpowers them—that it not only popularizes and persuades, but that it can actually produce behavioral change, including negative behavioral change, as well. This question of the effects of television (and other media too, for that matter) and how they are achieved has been studied repeatedly, yet a difficulty remains at the very heart of this subject. No one has been able to say authoritatively exactly what goes on in the moment of personal encounter—what transpires when the words and pictures move from the screen into the complex web of processes that comprise the individual consciousness. In fact, the vast majority of the inquiries have not even ventured into this area.

The reason for the gap in our knowledge is not hard to find. It has to do with the nature of all communications. Wilbur Schramm in a classic work (*The Process and Effects of Mass Communication*) describes the human communications system in its simplest terms as composed of a Source, Encoder, Signal, Decoder, and Destination. In personal communications the Source and Encoder are one person, and the Decoder and Destination are the other. The Signal is what is transmitted—words, pictures, images, gestures, signs, even silence. In mass communications, an organization is the Source and the Encoder—that is, it selects the words, pictures, sounds, signs, and whatever else may constitute the Signal, and transmits them. It tries to arrange them so that whoever it conceives to be its audience is able to decode them. In its simplest terms, this would mean using language that is common to most of its audience. This Schramm calls *group encoding.*

The problem in determining effects is that, while there is group encoding, "there is only individual decoding." That is each reader, listener, or viewer is an individual. Each brings a unique set of characteristics to the experience, right up to the very instant at which the communication is encountered. In Schramm's terms, those characteristics are a combination of "personality, situation, and group influence." Whatever their sources, they provide a filter, or web of intervening variables. Each encounter is filtered through those variables. Therefore, in television, as with books, newspapers, speeches, or any other medium, no two encounters are ever exactly alike, even for the same person. Since the intervening variables differ for everyone, what is taken from the experience of viewing, reading, and so on is different for everyone. Because this crucial point is often overlooked or misunderstood, it needs to be emphasized. It is not the acts of viewing, reading, and so on that are different, but rather the manner in which each person cognitively processes the media material that managed to capture some part of his or her attention. Further, no one has ever been able to sort out how each of those factors conditions even one viewer's reactions.

This problem goes beyond media. There can never be one-to-one correspondence between physical reality and the perception of that reality, in any situation. There is no reason why content—the physical reality of it—should be processed, that is, put through the set of intervening factors, or otherwise reponded to as special, simply because it has arrived via television and not from the multitude of nonmedia sources also competing for attention. Yet that assumption is implicit in, if not actually the basis of, an enormous amount of the commentary on the medium. There is another distinction to be made. There are two aspects to any stimulus we encounter. There is the stimulus in its original form—the car on the street, the words on the page, the picture on the tube—and there is the same thing altered to a greater or lesser extent by having passed through the intervening variables of the individual whose attention it has caught. So the teenager and the unemployed worker both see a gorgeous blonde in a brand new convertible pass by. One sees in it everything he admires and hopes for, the other a symbol of deprivation and injustice. Same content, but radically different perceptions.

Consequently, it has not been possible to establish that "viewing this caused that to happen." This means that television has been neither convicted nor acquitted. Nonetheless, a great deal of the research reads as though the case for conviction has been made. There is clearly an intuitive appeal in defining television viewing as a direct cause-and-effect relationship, where the television set is considered to be a sort of printing press and the viewer the blank page.

The dispute might be no more than academic, except that it has a damaging side effect—a misunderstanding of what television can or should do. We have witnessed in the last decade a massive real-life example of where television that is too powerful can lead. In all of the commentary on the astonishing political changes in Eastern Europe and the Soviet Union, little has been said about one of the most intriguing aspects: the results of the largest media experiment in history. The regimes there enjoyed what cognitive specialists call *monopolistic preemption;* they controlled all the means of communication, top to bottom—all the content, all the production, and all the distribution, including television, presumed to be the most powerful medium ever devised, the medium that in America has been accused of causing declining reading scores, of usurping the role of parent, teacher, and cleric, of determining whom we elect, what we eat, and on which side our brains will grow the fastest.

Surely, control of this overpowering device would produce the desired social consequences. But it didn't. It turns out that it is not just what is on the screen, but also what is on the people's minds that counts. The greater the distance between the two, the less real contact there is. That is to say, television, like any other medium, works when it responds to real interests and real needs in the audience. When these are ignored, when content is dictated from above, without regard for the user's sensibilities, the set is just a shadow box or, even worse, an unwitting stage on which a farce is enacted: the all-powerful "communicator" becomes an object of ridicule.

Yet so persistent is the predisposition to assume television's omnipotent and uniformly negative social influences that it even led the National Institute of Mental Health astray. In 1982 the NIMH issued a report called "Television and Behavior." It concluded that watching violence on television leads to aggressive behavior, which understandably led to the social science community to take a closer look at the report. One thing that was immediately obvious was the admission by the authors that not a single one of the studies they reviewed for the report actually established more than a correlational linkage. How could all of the studies together prove what none of them individually did? The NIMH's answer to this was "convergence." Roughly, this means that if you keep reaching the same conclusion, it must be valid, irrespective of the means by which you've reached it.

That conclusion, valid or not, did have consequences. The August 1992 issue of *TV Guide* is a case in point. The lead article is "Is TV Violence Battering Our Kids?" Since the conclusion is already implicit in the title, it does not come as much of a surprise: "The overwhelming weight of scientific opinion how holds that televised violence is indeed responsible for a percentage of the real violence in our society."

It does not say what the percentage is or what kind of "real violence" was caused, because we do not know whether any percentage of society's "real violence" is produced by the viewing of televised violence. The NIMH report is cited as a major support for this conclusion. None of the studies it cited turned up evidence in the least suggesting causation. The connection, if any, that is referred to is not actual causation but correlation, a looser standard. A 1992 American Psychological Association report said: "Accumulated research clearly demonstrates a correlation between viewing violence and aggressive behavior—that is, heavy viewers behave more aggressively than light viewers. Children and adults who watch a large number of aggressive programs also tend to hold attitudes and values that favor the use of aggression to solve conflicts."

That sounds clear enough (though the report does not point out that these differences have been found to exist not only between heavy and light viewers of television violence but also between heavy and light viewers of television in general), but the bases of these correlations are usually not nearly as firm as the conclusions drawn from them. One characteristic problem is that what is classified for the purpose of the studies as aggression bears little resemblance to what has been shown on the screen. Obviously, researchers can't go around interviewing perpetrators after acts of serious violence; it is rare even to be able to observe subjects in much less violent behaviors that still might be labeled aggressive. The usual route is to compare attitudes toward aggression with viewing of violent programs and draw conclusions from that, without any knowledge whatsoever about how the subjects themselves actually behave. The question of why some people are more aggressive than others, and always have been, long before television or any other modern media existed, is not addressed, nor why there is less violence in, for example, Japan, although there is heavy viewing of violent programs. There are no clear answers to these questions, only general agreement that there are multiple causes, most of them unrelated to media—environment, background, peer pressure, genetics, and the like.

In the so-called television era, America has been conservative, liberal, then conservative again, and now perhaps is somewhere in between. It has witnessed both a baby boom and a falling birth rate. It has seen Big Labor and Big Capital, government intervention in the economy, and a free competitive market. It has seen boom and recession, permissive and restrictive behavioral philosophies, increasing secularization and religious rivival. It is not reasonable to propose any single cause for all this, let alone television. What can be said is that television is a prominent aspect of this very complex society, but surely not the maker of it.

Television's power as an advertising medium is sometimes cited in support of these arguments. It is said that people buy their ideas, lifestyles, value systems, and the like from what they see on television exactly as they buy their toothpaste, and for the same reason. Or at least "other people" do; the proponents of these theories generally exclude themselves from the list of victims. How happy advertisers would be if the mere fact of advertising a product—on television or anyplace else—was enough to guarantee its purchase. But, as advertisers know well, the customer makes a decision after the message is received. Far more often than not, it is not the decision the advertiser hoped for. And here we are dealing with purchase decisions—changing a brand of toothpaste, buying a car, trying an appliance—that are socially supported, approved of, and practical. This hardly establishes that these same viewers uncritically absorb and imitate content from the rest of the medium and certainly not acts of violence and other forms of severe antisocial behavior that are clearly disapproved, if not actually punishable by law. To assume that television is a one-directional impact machine is to assume something that is contrary to human nature.

We are not suggesting that the media are either powerless or do not affect our lives. Of course they do. Television's massive social presence can hardly be argued away. The point we are making is that television's obvious informational and emotive power has been incorrectly treated as a uniform thing—the direct result of whatever we conceive the message to be—without regard for the way in which individuals may decode it. People do not merely *re*act to media, they *inter*act with media. They bring to what they see on the screen their own experiences, their own information, their own values—the sum of what is their own persona. The ultimate effect on them is the result of a whole set of variables. We are living in an era of extraordinary developments in communications. It is important that as we probe deeper into the relationship between the individual and the media, we at least acknowledge the complexity of the task and develop rational criteria for the methodology and the conclusions we reach. Unfortunately, this approach has been the exception, not the rule, in the past. The penalty for not doing so is to go on identifying surrogate villains to explain what bothers us instead of the real ones, which are usually far more difficult—politically, financially and otherwise—to deal with.

The following excerpt and the diagram is from *Schramm's Process and Effects of Mass Communications.*

### Communication in Terms of Learning Theory

In order to fill in the picture [in regard to learning theory], it seems desirable to sketch the diagram of how communication looks to a psychologist of learning. Let's start with the diagram [Figure 5–1], then explain it.

The diagram isn't as complicated as it looks. Remember that time in the diagram moves from left to right, and then follow the numbers and you won't get far off the road.

Begin with (1). This is the input. At the message level we have a collection of objectively measurable signs *s*. These come to your sense organs, where they constitute a stimulus for action. This stimulus we call (*s*). When the process gets as far as (*s*) you are paying attention. The message has been accepted. It may not have been accepted as intended; *s* may not equal (*s*); the sensory mechanism may have seen or heard it incompletely. But everything else that happens as a result of the message in that particular destination will now necessarily be the result of the stimulus accepted by your sense organs.

Now look at number (2). The message may not have to go to any other level in order to bring about a response. If a man waves his fist near your nose, you may dodge. If he squeezes your hand,

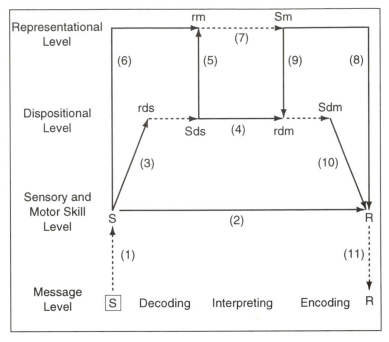

Figure 5.1 Communication and Learning Theory*

you may say "ouch!" These are learned, almost automatic, responses on the sensory and motor skill level.

But the stimulus may also bring about other kinds of activity within your nervous system. Look at number (3). The stimulus (*s*) may be translated into a grammatical response on your dispositional level—by which we mean the level of learned integrations (attitudes, values, sets, etc.) which make it so easy for you to dispose of the variety of stimuli that come to you in the course of a day. These are what we call the intervening variables. Suppose the stimulus stirs up activity in this area of intervening variables. Two things may happen. Look at number (4). The response may be so well learned that it doesn't even have to go to the level of thinking. You hear a line of a poem, and almost

*For the model Dr. Schramm is indebted to his colleague Dr. Charles E. Osgood.

automatically say the second ·line. In that case the activity is through numbers (4) and (10).

More often, however, the activity goes through number (5). Here the original stimulus has been decoded into grammar, fed through the intervening variables, and sent up to the representational level of the central nervous system, where meanings are assigned and ideas considered. Occasionally a stimulus comes to that level without going through the intervening variables—as in number (6). These stimuli create activity in the central nervous system (*rm*) which is the terminus of the decoding part of the process. This is equivalent to the meaning or significance of the signs *s*. What happens in number (7), then, is what we have been referring to as interpretation. The response *rm* which we call meaning becomes in turn a stimulus which sets the encoding process in action, so that (7) is both the terminus of decoding and the start of encoding. We learn to associate meanings with desired responses. And so the encoding process moves through (8) or (9). That is, we give certain orders which either pass directly to the neuro-muscular system (through 8) or are passed through the intervening variables (through 9 and 10). In any case, all this activity of the nervous system finally results in a response on the motor skill level (*r*), which results in output (number 11). If the output is an overt response (*R*), then we have another message, which may offer itself as a collection of sings *s* and be accepted by still another person as a stimulus (*s*).

This is what we believe happens when someone says to you, "Cigarette?" and you answer "Yes, please," or "No, thanks."

# Chapter *6*

## The Future

## The Distribution Explosion

Thirty years after the "wasteland" speech, at least one aspect of television is vastly different. Three channels became five, then seven, then twenty, then fifty. Now announcements are being made promising 500 channels. Additionally, the development of the videocassette recorder provided an infinite variety of choices of programs. In actuality, the VCR may be considered to be a channel with unlimited capacity.

But this explosion in means of distribution has not been accompanied by a corresponding growth in production. This has led to an increasing imbalance in the production-distribution-funding cycle. So the question becomes: What happens when one of these functions grows out of all proportion to the others?

It seems to us that each new possibility has to be considered in terms of its relationship to the fundamental business equation—the production-distribution-funding cycle—since it will remain in force no matter what else changes. In that respect, it should be recognized that two of the critical components here cannot undergo the expansion that has occurred in distribution. One of these is the creative process, and the other is the dimension in which all media operate—time.

## Time as the Controlling Factor

The successful inventions of the centuries have been those that were efficient time savers. This is true whether the invention was for the factory, the home, the farm, or the classroom. The Industrial Revolution saved hours of time by replacing manual labor in the home with machine labor in the factory. During this century, the inventions that succeeded were also those that were able to improve the use of time. For example, automobiles are faster than horses, airplanes faster than boats, jet aircraft faster and more efficient than propeller-driven aircraft. Electric utensils, washing machines, and stove freed women from the slavery of the open hearth, allowing them more time for other activities. The computer is also a major saver of time in offices and homes, and it provides more useful information more rapidly than other methods.

It is also true that despite the ability to save time, or allow it to be used more efficiently, new technology does not necessarily replace the old. Jet aircraft have not completely replaced propeller-driven planes, there are ocean liners still crossing the Atlantic despite supersonic transports, and the microwave oven has not replaced the kitchen stove.

In the world of entertainment, more than sixty years after the advent of television, radio still exists, and going to the movies is still a pleasant diversion from life's other requirements.

New technologies usually compete with more than one preceding technology, and their effects are not always easy to predict. For example, the videocassette recorder had a bigger impact on movies and pay television than on broadcast television. Cassette rentals and sales are now a larger share of movie revenues than box-office receipts. And movie viewers no longer have to commit themselves for an entire month of a pay service when they can rent what they want when they want it. On the other hand, the development of individual movies on demand at home, as it evolves, will have a serious impact on the video store.

Shopping at home, like catalogs, may save time by eliminating travel, but whether the present very limited inventory can be expanded is still in question.

Bigger savings of time may result from the evolution from hardwired locations to wireless conections. The use of wireless telephones, televisions, and facsimiles, enabling people to send and receive entertainment and information more effectively, in many cases may free up time for other purposes.

What will not change is the time it takes to either produce or consume entertainment. Despite more rapid communications and more avenues of communication, a play by Shakespeare or a concert of Bach or Beethoven cannot be shortened. Even more critical is the intractability of the creative process. The time it takes to create the story and write the movie, the book, the play, or the television program will not change. Similarly, even though more efficient production techniques continue to evolve, the coast of creating, performing, and producing professional entertainment programs is a function of supply and demand in a severely limited marketplace. It will continue to be very expensive, because the best talents will always be in short supply.

In sum, the multiplication of distribution channels where there is a finite amount of leisure time, a finite audience pool, and finite funding for production can only result in a world of limitless reruns.

## (DBS) Direct Broadcasting by Satellite

Everything we have stated about the proliferation of cable channels applies to direct broadcasting of programs from satellites to the home. Distribution of more channels similar in content to those carried by existing cable channels, without the benefit of local station's programming, will face severe marketing difficulties.

As stated previously, the value of network programs is enhanced by the association with the programs of local affiliates. One program source, without the other, diminishes both.

Because there is nothing unique regarding program content, DBS will be a very limited service.

## Telephone Companies and Television

Now that the regional telephone companies are going to be allowed to distribute programs as an inducement to put fiber optics into the home, the production imbalance problem will be exacerbated. As we have seen more channels does not necessarily mean more different programs. Historically, it has meant more repeats. The introduction of fiber optics with greater channel capacity poses a threat not to the networks, but to cable companies that have prospered through free access to broadcasters' schedules and to video rental stores. Once it is possible for a customer to rent a movie by phone and watch it at the his or her convenience, the need for video stores will diminish.

From the broadcasters' viewpoint, how their programs get into the home should be transparent. It does not matter whether the signal reaches the home screen via rooftop antenna, cable, or fiber optic, or whether it is taped and played at a later time. It is the attractiveness of the programming that will determine success or failure, not the means of transmission.

An overcapacity in distribution will be a self-correcting mechanism in a free market. The correction will be in the form of business failures, as new channels prove unable to attract the revenues required to sustain themselves.

## Menus and Schedules

The argument between the old and the new technologies is sometimes reduced to a single concept—menus versus schedules. A schedule is a preset sequence that the user must join in progress—rather like catching a train. The viewer must either wait until 7:00 P.M. Sunday to watch *60 Minutes* or arrage to tape it then for viewing later. Either way, the viewer must act on the basis of the scheduled time. A menu is a preexisting list that the viewer uses to choose the product. This week's edition of *60 Minutes* would be available for viewing or taping all week long. it could be tuned in on command.

Only a system with enormous storage capacity and almost unlimited avenues of access can offer a truly extensive menu, since lots of programs must be distributed simultaneously. The heart of the case for 500 channels lies in this capacity. The theory is that this makes all times prime time.

One caveat here is that prime time is not a purely arbitrary arrangement imposed on the viewers by traditional methods of broadcasting. It is there, and it has survived because it has important advantages to the audience as well as the broadcaster. Established programs standing side by side support each other. Putting new programs between older ones guarantees they will be sampled. There are also psychological and sociological aspects connected with viewing in the evening hours. Those leisure hours were not created for prime time; they already existed. Prime time was created for them. This is not a national habit by accident. The risks involved in the dismemberment of this process are rarely mentioned in stories about the new electronic highways.

How would a *60 Minutes* come into being if it were simply another title in a long list? *60 Minutes* was originally an unknown quantity. Placing it in the network schedule meant that millions of viewers were fed into it every week. Even so, it was still several years before it took hold. It was originally televised on Tuesday night at 10:00 P.M., but a scheduling problem and low ratings resulted in a move to Sunday at 6:00 P.M. When an entertainment program failed at 7:00 P.M., almost as a desperation move and because of the new requirement of the PTAR, *60 Minutes* was rescheduled to 7:00 P.M. The rest as the saying goes, is history! In 1993, the grogram elebrated its twenty-fifth anniversary.

Another classic example of the influence of a schedule is provided by an interview with Glen Charles, one of the creators of *Cheers,* in a May 9, 1993, *New York Times* piece about the shows history. Introduced in 1981, *Cheers* went nowhere at first, as Mr. Charles explains: "There were times when I thought we couldn't possibly survive . . . but the reviews were great and the audience we did have seemed to love the show. So we figured at least it wouldn't be an embarrassment to put on our resumes." The article goes on to say: "The show was helped by NBC's desperate state in the early 80's. . . . With no shows high in the ratings, NBC thought it might as well hang on to the one show it had that was getting good ink. Then NBC found *The Cosby Show,* and it brought hordes of viewers to Thursday nights. Many of them discovered *Cheers,* and the series shot heavenward in the ratings."

This structural-support system of an edge-to-edge program schedule is the most effective and efficient means yet devised for coping with the inevitable high rate of program failure. Strong programs pass their circulation on to new entries and success is prolonged by good positioning. Movies, plays, and books have to build their own markets every time out, but the *60 Minutes* crowd is there, waiting, every Sunday at seven.

The continuous audience flow of a network schedule—millions of viewers, hour after hour, day after day—with thousands of promotional announcements washing over each of its programs is a bounty that would not exist in a pure "menu" world. Would these same programs, detached from that process, outside the stream, ever have achieved the same popularity? How would they have been introduced—one at a time, five at a time, ten at a time? Would series, especially those with continuous plot lines, exist at all? Could television become single feature–oriented, like the movies, where $10 or $15 million has to be spent promoting every single title? And who would provide the funds? Not advertisers, who need a guaranteed audience in advance. Not viewers, who are unfamiliar with the product. Not producers or distributors, who need speedy returns. There are many unresolved questions relating to both supply and demand about the menu concept. However it evolves, it does not seem to us that is will displace the networks' schedules.

Another factor not widely recognized is that the five hundred-channel world is a cable-inspired concept conjured up when cable growth came to a halt. The idea seems to be "If we can't grow by penetration, then we'll grow by proliferation." But the difference is that one is expansive and the other is divisive. A 500-channel world is one in which 490 niche services will fight each other over ever smaller audience fragments. In fact, that is already beginning to happen. It has nothing to do with why people watch *60 Minutes*.

### Expansion and Its Limits

As they are now being presented, both the five hundred-channel world and the electronic superhighway appear to be supply-side concepts in that they presume that demand will follow supply. The intriguing question is whether the demand will come simply from shifting an existing source to a newer one—for example, movies move from the local video rental store to an on-line pay-per-view service, in which case the market does not actually expand—or whether there will be an actual increase in total viewers and expenditures.

Demand in practical terms means something more than desire. In order to match demand with supply, certain qualificatons have to be met. Sufficient numbers of people need to have the interests, the needs, the available time, the economic status, and the intellectual capacity to make use of the outputs of these systems.

In some cases, we know more or less who these people are—moviegoers, videocassette renters, computer owners, software buyers of different sorts and so on. But since the whole point of the new electronic era is that the output will be vastly greater than it is now, demand will have to increase, if it is to be supported. This can occur in two ways: (1) through greater usage by established segments; (2) by adding new users.

In the case of movies it means that the people who rent videocassetes will now order up more movies, and/or people who do not rent them will now begin to do so. In both cases this means that more money and more time will be spent watching movies at home. Since it is very difficult to arbitrarily increase movie production by a significant degree, these people must become more willing to sample product than they are now. Will convenience alone do that?

The next question is where the increases in time and money will come from. The day cannot be expanded, and there is no indication that the work week is likely to get shorter. This means some other activity will have to be forgone. If disposable income does not grow, then people must give up some existing expenditure in order to pay for more movie viewing.

These questions surround a relatively simple and well-established marketplace. Movies are already being viewed extensively in the home. In fact, home video rentals are now the largest single source of revenue for movies. All we are talking about here is a new means of distribution. These same questions, plus other, apply where wholesale changes are anticipated. A much discussed example is the transfer of mail-order catalogs to the video screen. Here the questions begin at an earlier stage: Does someone accustomed to picking up the L. L. Bean catalog at random wish to do something similar on a home screen? Is flipping around in the glossy, familiar landscape of duck hunting boots and plaid shirts while sitting in an armchair burdensome or pleasurable? What does the screen add? Does it save time? Can it carry as many items? Is it easier to use? Does it make the product more attractive? Would a host and live pictures do so? What are the economics of the move? Is that kind of effort affordable to Bean or to the presenting channel? It is rare for a televised picture, no matter where it is generated, to cost less than producing an equivalent printed page. That means it has to return more sales per dollar invested, either through increased circulation or more sales per customer, or both.

Again, here we are talking about a well-defined, long-established market, whose general characteristics are well known, yet it is full of imponderables. The further we move away from the known markets, the more difficult the questions become.

In the face of all the evidence we have, there is a widely held belief that greater availability of information and improved presentation is going to trigger an increase in educational uses of the screen. A wave of autodidacticism will set in, with people studying lessons, doing homework, and getting individual responses at home. This scenario is often extended to the view that self-improvement will win out over *60 Minutes* or *Murphy Brown* or *Oprah*. Our own belief is that this is not a question of technology, but of human nature.

The outcome is not difficult to predict. History tells us that, given a choice, the audience will opt for relaxation at the end of a tiring day. They will seek to be entertained for the same reasons they have done so during the eight decades that broadcasting has existed.

## The Future of Network Evening News Broadcasts

Any consideration of the future of the three major network news programs has to begin with an understanding of their history, and particularly their relationship to the local news broadcasts that precede them in individual markets.

Network television evening news got under way in the early 1950s when CBS presented a fifteen-minute program, simply produced, with an anchorman reading about worldwide developments that occurred during the previous twenty-four hours. NBC, then ABC, eventually created their own evening news programs. In 1963, CBS expanded its program to thirty minutes, and this action was eventually copied by NBC and ABC.

During the 1950s, 1960s, and the early 1970s, news stories were all on film. And film, by its very nature, took time to process and develop. Because handling film is a time-consuming process and its cost is high, there were not a lot of film stories in local broadcasts. On the other hand, because of the number of foreign and domestic bureaus at the networks, a network would often find it had collected more foreign and national filmed stories than it could use. During the editing process these were said to wind up "on the cutting room floor."

By the 1960s, when network news had been expanded to a half hour, and most local programs had followed suit, the affiliates, who lacked the resources for foreign coverage and had only limited access to national stories, began to request that unused stories be sent to them for use in local programs. These activities gradually became formalized into nightly *feeds*, with numbers of unused network stories transmitted electronically directly to the affiliates on a scheduled basis.

In hindsight, at this point the networks should have expanded the evening news to one hour. They had the stories to fill the time, the stations' request meant the stories had value, and the Prime Time Access Rule had not yet restricted the amount of time the networks could use in the evening slot. There is a good chance the one-hour news could have been done, and once it was in place, it would beve been diffcult to rule it out of existence.

A change in the local/network news structure and relationship occurred in the mid-1970s with the development of Electronic News Gathering (ENG), a method of collecting stories without using film. Because the method was electronic, local and network news organizations could tape as many stories as they believed were important and not worry about development time. Also, electronic TV news crews required fewer people, so stations were able to afford more crews. More crews meant more stories, which led to longer local news programs. Many local stations expanded to an hour, and some even programmed two hours of news. As part of this expansion, the affiliates developed a need for more stories from the network to use in the local broadcasts.

By the 1990s, local stations were providing news about local, national, and international events, sometimes for more than one hour prior to the network's evening news broadcasts. This development has caused some observers to believe that because of the redundancy, the evening news programs of the three networks will eventually disappear.

We believe this does not have to happen, but in this changed environment the networks clearly need to reexamine the mission of the evening news. One would expect that the point is to distinguish these services from their local counterparts. Unfortunately, the networks appear to be copying local presentations and, in so doing, losing much of their reason to exist.

The networks need to ask these questions: "What if there were no network program but everything else existed as it now does? What kind of broadcast would be done if the network were just beginning an evening news in the midst of all of the local programming?"

One possible response would be to move toward a more thought-provoking broadcast, one that would add to the headlines, not just recount them, and would challenge the viewer to think more seriously about important issues. A program that by its intelligence and quality of presentation would be intellectually stimulating. A program that could be a platform for the expression of conflicting opinions. Since television cannot show a picture of an idea, this type of broadcast would showcase the intellectual capabilities of the network correspondents and their special guests. In sum, it would feature news, issues, conflict, and stimulation, in one well-paced program. In essence, it would be a broadcast that was original, not a copy; it would be a complement to the local news; it would fill a national need; and, ultimately, it would be a compliment to the network news division.

## *The Future of Public Broadcasting*

This following quotation is from "The Report of the Twentieth-Century Fund Task Force on Public Television" issued in 1993.

> Public television was created in the late 1960's as an alternative to the "vast wasteland" of commercial television. Over the years, much has changed. Television has become even more central to the American experience. The wasteland, to be sure, has not been reclaimed, but today's public broadcasters are being swept along by revolutionary developments. Satellites, cable, pay-per-view, niche programming, and the prospect of 500 channels are drastically altering the environment for all televison. For public television, embroiled in controversies over "balance" in its programming and pressured by economic necessity that has led to increased commercialization, the changing landscape raises the

most basic question of all: Is there still a need for noncommercial television as we know it?

One can also take this question a step further and ask it in the politically incorrect form: Was there ever a need for non-commercial television? And if there was, how large and how deep was that need? Eliminating commercials does not eliminate questions of supply and demand. There still must be a marketplace for the product, even if it is simply defined by time spent watching. In our view, public television is not so much the story of an endangered mission as an impossible one, because it is based on extremely fragile propositions.

One is an exaggerated notion of television's natural pedagogical possibilities, the idea that the tube was going to be the long sought for magic classroom, where information and entertainment at last joined hands and lived happily ever after. There is, in fact, only a very narrow strip of activity where this is possible, *Sesame Street* being perhaps the best example. It is a brilliant, but limited achievement that has not proven to be expandable. Yet PBS is expected to deal with a full network schedule. Clearly, as America prepares for the twenty-first century, the critical question regarding the need for a PBS system receives different responses from different observers.

At a June 1993 television conference in Banff, Canada, underwritten primarily by grants from the Government of Alberta and the Government of Canada, and attended by an international array of senior industry figures, one of the topics was "The Crisis in Public Broadcasting." That it was felt to be necessary to address the topic using the word *crisis* is indicative of the seriousness of the issue. The questions posed at the conference included: What is public television's role in a multimedia environment? Can it be distinctive? Can it compete? Can it survive? What are the political, cultural, and economic implications? There were no clear answers—if there had been any, there would have been no need for such a dialogue. Most of the discussion concerned finding ways to cut the cost of production by developing transnational joint-programming ventures.

If one accepts the original premise for public TV as an alternative to commercial television, then the contemporary issue is that there are now plenty of other alternatives, including much of what was formerly associated with noncommercial TV. For example, The Discovery Channel, The Learning Channel, The American Movie Channel, Arts & Entertainment, Nickelodeon, and The History Channel provide much of the material that was once almost exclusively the domain of public television in America. In 1994, it is a specious argument to defend the need for PBS on the basis of the *Civil War* or the *MacNeil/Lehrer Newshour*. In the history of television, it has been demonstrated that programs that deserve to be made and broadcast eventually are. The error is more often in the opposite direction. Because of the unceasing demand for more and more product to try to fill the insatiable appetite required by the twenty-four hour TV schedule, programs of questionable quality are being scheduled that in simpler times would never have been produced. PBS is not immune to this; otherwise why would they show reruns of Lawrence Welk, Ed Sullivan, Bikini Beach Blanket movies, and others of that ilk? In addition, the easy availability of videos through schools, libraries, and stores has made many "PBS-type" programs for all ages accessible to millions of viewers.

One result of the proliferation of competitive product on other channels is that the audience to public TV has decreased. The same report noted above points out that the PBS average rating went from a 2.7 in 1987 to a 2.1 in 1991. Smaller audiences mean ever greater pressure on fund-raising requirements. This leads to a futher dilemma. In an effort to reach more viewers and, hopefully, more donors, the temptation is to schedule programs that have a broader appeal—that is, to emulate the services to which PBS is supposed to be the alternative. While this may help the bottom line, it does raise the question of why taxpayer dollars should be used to help underwrite programs on public television that are "free" on commercial television and some cable channels. It is possible that a large part of PBS's current problem stems from its very beginning and the philosophy underlying its creation.

It is certainly questionable whether in the minds of the viewing audience commercial broadcasting ever was the "vast wasteland" some critics believed it to be, and whether large numbers of viewers ever felt a compelling need for an alternative. After all, it was commercial television that presented the *Hallmark Hall of Fame, Playhouse 90, Studio One, The Young People's Concerts, Captain Kangaroo, CBS Reports, 60 Minutes, Face the Nation, Meet the Press, U.S. Steel Hour, Armstrong Circle Theater, Walt Disney Presents, General Electric College Bowl, Camera Three,* and *Discovery,* along with the comedic talents of Jack Benny, Groucho Marx, Burns and Allen, Red Skelton, Jackie Gleason, Sid Caesar, and Lucille Ball, among others, as well as world-scale news and public events coverage.

In light of this, it is interesting to observe that the same era in which television was referred to as a vast wasteland by a former FCC commissioner is now looked upon by many broadcast historians as the Golden Age of Television. This seeming paradox may explain why a large segment of the viewing audience never understood what public broadcasting, in the broader sense, was all about.

The role of public broadcasting is further complicated by the differences in ownership of public TV stations. An analysis of 175 specific licensees that operate 351 local stations shows that 86 are owned by community organizations, 55 are owned by colleges or universities, 23 are owned by statewide authorities, and 11 are owned by local educational or municipal authorities. And each has a different mission. In this complicated environment, it is understandable that programs from these stations fail to achieve broad circulation. Many of them are simply not designed for that end. Furthermore, a mass audience is not aware of their availability. However, it is the American taxpaying population that contributes more than $250 million each year toward PBS programs. Based on circulation figures, it appears that the masses are paying for programs watched by the few.

The challenges facing public broadcasting exist in other countries also. The British Broadcasting Corporation, long used as the model of what government-supported broadcasting should be, is also suffering. During the summer of 1993, the audience to BBC programs was 43 percent, down from 51 percent in 1981 and less than the audience to independent television. BBC1, the primary channel, has about 28 percent of the audience, compared to 41 percent for Independent Channel 3.

Also in 1993, the Canadian Government planned to try to cut $250 million from its allocation to the CBC by the year 1995. This would be in addition to an $108-million cut that took place in 1991–92. As a result of that reduction, the CBC closed eleven television stations. So the financial difficulties facing public television are not confined to the United States.

The fact that the BBC programs carried on PBS have an aura of high quality about them is often interpreted as an indictment of American programming, but commercial programs produced in the United States have become the standard by which other programs around the world are measured.

The popularity of American commercial programs overseas has led governments to attempt to limit their number. The issue has become a trade problem, most notably in France. The argument over quality has an abstract dimension that can never be resolved, but it is abundantly clear that no foreign source feels able to compete with U.S. product. There is an interesting case of cultural cross-referencing here. *Dallas*, an American soap opera, was immensely popular in Britain, far more so than *Upstairs, Downstairs,* a "quality" BBC soap opera of the same era. *Upstairs, Downstairs* did enjoy a successful run on PBS here, but at a circulation far below that of the popular American programs of its time. Quality is in the eye of the beholder.

Because public TV in other countries has strong audience identification, the question of why public television in America has not been as popular here can be raised. One answer might be that the foreign television services often had no serious competition. Another may be that American commercial television has carried out its government mandate to operate in the "public interest, convenience and necessity," better than many TV critics believe. Specifically, the legal requirement of the communications act that commercial stations must fulfill has resulted in an abundance of local news, public affairs broadcasts, and coverage of community activities regarding arts and culture, to a degree that is unmatched by any other broadcasting endeavor.

If public broadcasting in America is facing critical times, one cause is an imbalance among creation, distribution, and funding needs. The cost of creating programs with high production values continues to climb, while the audience required to support the costs continues to shrink. With revenues declining, some public television stations have taken steps that appear to be well outside the original mandate, such as accepting commercials and resorting to home-shopping programs.

In the fall of 1993, WTTW, the major public broadcasting station in Chicago, began testing a shopping service with the hope that a percentage of the sales would provide more programming revenues. The experiment ended shortly after it began.

In another attempt at revenue enhancement, a former president of PBS suggested that commercial broadcasters should be charged a fee for using the spectrum, and those funds should be used to underwrite PBS costs—a strategy originally recommended by the study group mentioned above that was hired to analyze the plight of public broadcasting in America.

The spectrum fee issue caused one trade publication to note that the real issue is not "whether broadcasters should be required to pay for a competitor's programming, but whether the whole country should be required to involuntarily support an idea past its prime." There are also those who argue that public television inevitably caters to the elite and ask why taxpayer dollars should be used to support such a system.

This was a major topic of discussion in 1993 before congressional funding approval was received, and it will be a major issue in 1996, when the congressional approval will again be needed. Unless those who operate the public broadcasting system can demonstrate more clearly what unique values are inherent in a taxpayer-subsidized service, further approval will be very difficult to obtain.

It is undeniable that the same economic "laws" that govern all television communications affect PBS. In an effort to address the future and maintain long-term viability, the Public Broadcasting Service will have to take steps to generate much greater revenues in ways other than spectrum fees. Since cable channels that compete with all broadcasting stations and offer similar programs found on PBS do not use the spectrum, to charge only commercial broadcasters a fee to support PBS would be discriminatory and very controversial.

The cable channels that offer "PBS type" programs in some cases receive two sources of funds: advertising revenues, and, when tiered in some systems, subscription fees. In the case of subscription fees, the audience may not be watching, but the fees will still be generated. Since PBS does not have either of these income streams, it is competing for programs on what could be considered an uneven playing field. In one effort to offset this handicap, it has resorted to acquiring programs originally produced for other networks at lower, "repeat" costs.

The series, "I'll Fly Away," produced for commercial television, was picked up by PBS, after cancellation by NBC.
*Source:* NBC

The BBC programs carried by PBS are the best example of this. More recently, a critically acclaimed series canceled by NBC because of low viewership, *I'll Fly Away,* was acquired. Carrying reruns of American commercial programs again raises the question of the role of PBS in the multichanneled universe.

Unless there is a large increase in revenues, the problems affecting public television in the United States will become greater. If revenues suffer, programming suffers; if programming suffers, distribution suffers; if distribution suffers, circulations suffers. This situation has already begun. Since PBS charges stations for certain programs (unlike the commercial networks, which pay their affiliates to carry network shows), and since local PBS stations have their own financial difficulties, some stations have refused to pay the network and have substituted less expensive local programs for network shows. This lack of clearance further erodes the national audience to PBS. This cycle, if continued, becomes a death spiral: cheaper and lower-quality programs lead to smaller audiences; smaller audiences lead to smaller revenues; even smaller revenues lead to even cheaper programs and even smaller audiences. Thus the system devours itself.

The situation is not hopeless. It may be that the best future role for public television is to play a larger role in the continuing need for education at a local level. It is what stations owned by universities have been doing for decades. It is what ETV (Educational Television) is all about.

However, if the Public Broadcasting Service in the United States continues to attempt to provide a network service to 351 stations in an increasingly competitive communication complex without changing basic founding principles and beliefs, it will fail. Then the answer to the question posed in the PBS report, "Is there still a need for noncommercial television as we know it?" will be no.

Once that conclusion is reached, the status of 351 public broadcasting stations will dramatically change. With a change in current laws, some of the stations will be sold or will begin to accept comercials in direct competition to other channels in the market. Many of them may eventually become affiliated with one of the commercial networks.

And some of them, especially those associated with universities or supported by local funds, will become mere extensions of the classroom. This is educational television in its literal sense. The original ambition of PBS was to enliven and enlarge this usage, to take it off the campus and into the nation at large. When this has happened—the recent *Civil War* series is a case in point—it has been the exception. It is not sustainable.

In summary, public television was confined to small spaces by its very mandate and simultaneously handed the immense canvas of a full day's schedule. Thus, there was from the outset a mismatch between what was doable and what was asked to be done. The audience at large never has demonstrated anything like the appetite for the service that its ubiquitous presence implies. Does anyone believe that there would be a serious issue regarding the future of public television if the people who watch *60 Minutes* watched PBS? The constituency in that case would be its own justification. And now, that constituency, always slender, continues to be eaten away by a series of new competitors.

## High-Definition Television

The march toward a HDTV standard began in earnest in 1988, when the FCC announced its intention to choose a standard for advanced television and invited companies from around the world to propose systems. A testing phase began in 1991. In May of 1993 it was announced that the three remaining top rivals in the competition had agreed to join forces on a single approach. The system adopted will allow television stations to transmit programs with five different formats of progressive scanning—a new means of transmission whose format is compatible with computers—and one format of interlaced scanning, the means currently in use. Television stations will continue to broadcast on their present frequencies, but they will be given a second channel for high-definition transmission and will be required to begin using the second channel within five years of the adoption of the standard. New television sets capable of receiving the new type of signal are expected to become available as early as 1995.

In the minds of many in government, developing an American standard was a trade issue that could provide a needed boost for American TV set production. All current sets are manufactured by foreign companies. It was presumed that a shift to an accepted U.S. standard could mean more jobs for American workers.

At least in the early announcements of this development, what we see as a number of practical drawbacks were not emphasized. Note that the drive for HDTV did not begin with broadcasters, who ought to have a major interest in any significant enhancement of their product. They are aware that American technical standards have always been worse than European. In this country, the television picture consists of 525 lines, in Europe 625 lines. Despite a lower-quality picture, American programs are the standard of the world, proving that content is more important than technology. If, after testing, the new regulations are passed, American television stations will be required to spend an estimated $5 to $10 million each for transmitting and production equipment in order to maintain their license and the ability to operate. And the public will eventually have to purchase new sets at premium prices. Ultimately, the entire hardware chain—production, transmission, and reception—will have to be replaced, all because of a standard for which neither the American consumer nor the broadcaster has been clamoring.

Mr. Stuart "Red" Martin, a veteran broadcaster who is the owner of an extremely successful television station, made some interesting observations on this issue. He combines sophisticated engineering knowledge with business acumen, so his opinion deserves our respect on several grounds. He sees two enormous obstacles facing HDTV:

One [obstacle] is the installed base of receivers that cannot deal with the signal. The other is the current HDTV decision to move all HDTV broadcasting to the UHF band.

Japan provides a preview of the future of an incompatible HDTV system. In spite of a heavily financed, government-supported effort, including several hours of programming, the viewership has been dismal.

On the second point, someone has forgotten why so many UHF stations failed early on. The coverage is severely limited, because of the way UHF propagates. Should the FCC plan go into effect, there would be a loss of service to a very large faction of current viewers, particularly in urban (and hilly) areas. This would result in a major uproar and a serious political problem, not least because local television stations are the principal means by which politicians, particularly senators and congressmen, reach their constituencies.

The development of FM provides a useful parallel. Announced about 1938, it was an exact analog to HDTV. It was high-tech, high quality, high promise, and incompatible with existing sets. Nothing happened at all until WWII, when the army poured millions and millions into it to provide crystal-controlled FM communications for the tanks of the Armed Forces.

After the war, with this installed manufacturing base, a serious effort was made to market it. Several cash-heavy broadcasters built wide area coverage stations, figuring to simulcast AM broadcasts inexpensively and wait for the audience to develop (just as planned for HDTV today). The FCC threw a wrench into these plans by suddenly limiting allowed coverage, but, nevertheless, several major market stations persisted. One was WHDH in Boston, then a CBS affiliate. After three or four years they decided to test for audience by turning off the transmitter during the most popular show of the time (I think it was something like Tommy Dorsey, Tuesday at 10 P.M.). Not one single complaint was received. And this was when CBS Radio was at the height of its popularity.

Ultimately, HDTV will succeed or fail not by the choice of technology, but by the quality of the programs that are carried. Whether the signal is sharper or the picture larger will never be as important as the messages themselves. HDTV is not a revolutionary development like basic television was when it first began to serve the people. Rather, it is another evolutionary step on the road of continued engineering changes, like the advent of color TV, stereophonic sound, portable receivers, and miniature TV sets. The millions of dollars invested in the development of quality sound and pictures has little effect on whether the audience prefers *Murphy Brown* more than a Monday night movie, or *The Bill Cosby Show*, more than *The Simpsons*. In this regard, nothing has changed. With HDTV, it is possible that the only ones to gain financially will be the set manufacturers. And even that is not a certainty.

## Computers and Television

Another consideration in regard to the future is how computers will be used in the home. Much has been written about how the home computer will be combined with the television set to provide all kinds of marvelous opportunities in communications, from business uses to personal entertainment, from leisure time activities to educational and instructional uses. One of the more emphatic statements about this comes from George Gilder in his recent book *"Life After Television:* "Spoiled by what was long a captive audience, however, the television networks are sitting ducks for the telecomputer. They will rapidly discover that many of their most successful shows quickly will fail when faced with serious alternatives."

Gilder's thesis is that the new technology of the microchip

and fiber optics takes the program-making function away from the old providers—the makers of popular entertainment as we know it now—and puts it into the hands of individuals, who will be able to construct any sort of programming they disire. By "serious alternatives" Gilder means an almost limitless choice of interactive educational and informational activites.

At the heart of Gilder's position is the question of how technology interacts with human nature. He believes that millions of viewers will turn away from the "forced feeding" of network fare toward self-programmed "serious alternatives" as soon as they have the opportunity. "Television is a tool of tyrants", he says. "Its overthrow will be a major force for freedom and individuality, culture and morality. That overthrow is at hand."

Our view is that there is little to prevent that from happening right now, and that people watch today's programs because that is what they prefer to do, not because they have no alternatives. The thing that is most likely to replace a popular program is a more-popular program.

We believe that rather than one set of hardware being used for multiple purposes, multiple sets will be used for specific purposes. Computers, large ones, small ones, and portable ones, will be used for computing. Television sets, large ones, small ones, and portable ones, will be used for watching entertainment and informational programs, as they are today.

Gilder is certainly not alone in his belief that the television set and the computer will eventually merge. In fact, that seems to be the principal thesis underlying the FCC's recent approval of a high-definition television standard that includes a new scanning process for television signals adaptable for computer screens. If there is any hard research suggesting that large numbers of people would like to watch NFL football, movies, and their favorite situation comedies in the same place where they do their word processing or balance their checkbook, we are not aware of it. It seems unlikely to us. What is clear is that both television and computer manufacturing interests would dearly wish this to be the case, since an enormous new market would open up for both of them. The decisive point, however, is not their desires, but those of their customers.

The fundamental business issue in Gilder's position is whether the actual time spent with the two activities changes— that is, whether there will be a radical shift away from watching traditional television to self-constructed "serious alternatives." In that respect, the results of a Gallop poll published in the *New York Times* in May of 1993 are of interest. Americans were asked what they do with time they consider their own on each day of the week. The results were reported as percentages (Table 6–1).

Watching television ranged from a low of 26.2 percent on Sunday to a high of 34.1 percent on Thursday. It outranked the second-highest activity by a factor of three or four to one, so there really was nothing in second place. The two categories combined that seem to relate most closely to Gilder's "serious alternatives"— "Do-it-Yourself" and "Self-Improvement"— never got above 6 percent.

We see these numbers as representing not just activities, but appetites. We do not think that merging the screen or converging the world of information with the world of enter- tainment in a "telecomputer" will change the public's palate.

John Dickinson made some interesting comments on this topic in the September 1993 issue of *PC Computing* magazine, in a piece called "PC's and TV's: Do You Really Want to Run Apps with Vanna White?":

> It's easy enough to say that interactive television, for example, can become a substitute for computers in the home, and you can already watch TV on many PC's. What's not so easy to say is how we will use all of this.
>
> The problem is that computers and their users are infor- mation-intensive, while television and its users are entertain-

ment-intensive, and the audiences for each are fundamentally different. In general, information-hungry audiences tend to have special interests, which make them very focused on particular types of information about particular types of products. On the other hand, entertainment audiences tend to be broadly focused. As a result, television content has more mass appeal, while information services, such as online, have content designed for special interest groups.

We would add that this distinction applies not only to the two types of audiences but even within them: the person who spends time with both devices still seeks separate satisfactions from them more than likely in separate spaces.

This point was addressed in an article in the *New York Times* in which four writers with expertise in this area commented on the prospects for the predicted electronic superhighway. One of them, James Gleick, a science writer, had this to say: "My television set is still sitting there, all by itself in the kitchen. . . . And my computer is somewhere else altogether. Telephone companies and cable-television companies may not be able to keep their hands off each other, but blending our actual telephones and televisions will surely require a lot more than FCC approval."

All the evidence shows that the majority of people will spend far more time with entertainment than with information. It is by no means clear that the fifty million people who watch the networks' prime-time schedules are also 50 million potential interactive users—that the prime-time audience ball of thread can simply be unwound into separate interactive strands. Moreover, the economics of special-interest programming on television are far more forbidding than the economics of special-interest programming for computers.

The issue, then, is the difference between what technology can provide and what users want. In the 1960s, media critic/philosopher Marshall McLuhan originated the concept of the

TABLE 6–1. At Leisure: Americans' Use of Down Time

Thursday is a big day for fishing. Sunday is water skiing day. Every day is television day.

Americans were asked to explain what they do with time they consider their own. Time spent doing things they felt obliged to do—jobs, sleep, commuting, child care, cooking, household chores, etc.—was not included. (However, some said they cooked, shopped, or did yard work for fun.) Only activities taking at least one percent of leisure time are shown. Others that were named, including sex, and collecting barbed wire, did not meet that standard.

The percentages shown are for time spent on each activity, not the number of people who do it.

| Monday 5.41 hours (%) | | Tuesday 5.13 hours (%) | | Wednesday 5.34 hours (%) | | Thursday 5.06 hours (%) | |
|---|---|---|---|---|---|---|---|
| Watching television | 33.1 | Television | 33.3 | Television | 30.2 | Television | 34.1 |
| Socializing (on phone, in person) | 7.1 | Socializing | 7.1 | Reading | 6.0 | Reading | 7.4 |
| Reading | 6.0 | Reading | 6.4 | Socializing | 5.6 | Socializing | 6.9 |
| Do-it-yourself projects | 3.5 | Do-it-yourself | 3.7 | Do-it-yourself | 4.4 | Do-it-yourself | 4.0 |
| Shopping | 2.6 | Time outdoors | 3.0 | Shopping | 2.5 | Time outdoors | 2.8 |
| Time outdoors (rest, recreation) | 2.1 | Shopping | 2.9 | Hobbies | 2.4 | Shopping | 2.7 |
| Gardening | 2.0 | Hobbies | 2.3 | Time outdoors | 1.6 | Hobbies | 2.0 |
| Vacation | 1.6 | Sewing, knitting | 2.1 | Self-improvement | 1.6 | Yard work/maintenance | 1.8 |
| Golf | 1.5 | Yard work/maintenance | 2.0 | Sewing, knitting | 1.1 | Fishing | 1.3 |
| Yard work/maintenance | 1.2 | Self improvement (study, counseling) | 1.6 | Vacation | 1.1 | Sewing, knitting | 1.1 |
| Sewing, knitting | 1.2 | Team Sports | 1.2 | Yard work/maintenance | 1.0 | Golf | 1.0 |
| Team sports | 1.0 | Gardening | 1.2 | | | | |
| Parlor sports | 1.0 | Golf | 1.0 | | | | |
| Hobbies | 1.0 | | | | | | |

| Friday 5.29 hours (%) | | Saturday 6.99 hours (%) | | Sunday 7.39 hours (%) | |
|---|---|---|---|---|---|
| Television | 28.7 | Television | 26.6 | Television | 26.2 |
| Socializing | 8.9 | Socializing | 8.4 | Socializing | 8.3 |
| Reading | 4.6 | Shopping | 6.1 | Reading | 4.3 |
| Do-it-yourself | 4.0 | Do-it-yourself | 5.0 | Time outdoors | 3.4 |
| Shopping | 2.6 | Reading | 4.6 | Religious activities | 2.7 |
| Eating out | 2.2 | Time outdoors | 3.3 | Vacation | 2.1 |
| Watching a movie | 2.1 | Swimming | 1.6 | Shopping | 2.0 |
| Vacation | 1.8 | Vacation | 1.5 | Do-it-yourself | 2.0 |
| Time outdoors | 1.6 | Golf | 1.4 | Volunteer work | 1.8 |
| Gardening | 1.5 | Eating out | 1.3 | Eating at home | 1.7 |
| Sewing, knitting | 1.3 | Watching a movie | 1.3 | Gardening | 1.7 |
| Self-improvement | 1.3 | Fishing | 1.2 | Hobbies | 1.5 |
| Team sports | 1.2 | Gardening | 1.2 | Water skiing | 1.4 |
| Hobbies | 1.1 | Cooking, baking | 1.1 | Swimming | 1.3 |
| Spectator sports | 1.1 | Hobbies | 1.0 | Eating out | 1.2 |
| Swimming | 1.1 | Team sports | 1.0 | Watching a movie | 1.1 |
| | | | | Fishing | 1.1 |
| | | | | Team sports | 1.1 |
| | | | | Spectator sports | 1.1 |

*Source: Leisure Trends* compilation of Gallup data, a telephone survey of more than 6,000 Americans aged 16 and older conducted June 1990 through June 1992.

Reprinted with permission of *American Demographics* magazine.

global village. He saw television as an extension of the electronic pathways of our own physiology. It gave our eyes and ears unlimited range, turning the planet into a village.

It is an appealing idea. We think of a village as a community that is within our personal grasp. We walk about in it. We recognize its people, homes, shops. It is friendly, familiar, unthreatening. The globe was to be reduced to these dimensions by a medium that could transmit sights and sounds from any given point to any other given point. People in a village in Montana could look in on people in a village in Ghana, and vice versa. The assumption was that they would come to recognize and understand each other.

But, as Professor W. Russell Neuman, of Tufts University, points out in an article in the *New Yorker,* the people in Montana might not be very interested in the village in Ghana. What television has actually given us, he says, is a common space, and, he adds, "it turns out to be dominated by Arnold Schwarzenegger and Bette Midler, not an African village."

That is not to say the McLuhan's vision of globally shared experience has not happened. Certainly television has greatly increased our awareness of remote cultures and events. But there is a difference between extended consciousness as a philosophical/sociological matter and attention as a matter of personal priority. In a market where choice exists, what counts is attention. The shared concern is self-interest. The people in the village in Montana and the people in the village in Ghana will be interested first in what is going on around them. In America that means what the weather forecast is, what traffic conditions are, what has happened in an area that connects with their experience. In the ordinary course of things, their interest in news will diminish with distance. Moreover, their interest in news in general will be limited. They will spend a far greater amount of time on entertainment.

All of this points again to the dichotomy between the capacities of technology and the inclinations of human nature. It is a point that we have returned to throughout this book because it is the one that underlies everything put on the screen, and understanding it is of paramount concern in an era where technology is being treated as an end in itself.

We see each part of the production, distribution, and funding process as being analogous to one leg of a three-legged stool. It is easy to understand what happens when one of the legs is out of balance with the others. This is why we view the five hundred-channel future, a huge extension of one of the legs, with skepticism. Given the fact that the audience is at any given point finite, and that it is difficult to see how the present seven-hour television day can be significantly enlarged, the endless addition of channels can only lead to an endless subdivision of viewing, in which more and more offerings fight over fewer and fewer users. Here it is not the technology but the economics that become decisive.

### The Fate of the Networks

One of the more fascinating occurrences during Gene's eleven years as president, and certainly one of the most publicized, was Ted Turner's attempt to take over CBS. One day, Bill Leonard, the president of News, called him and asked what he thought about buying CNN. Gene told him it would be interesting to consider and asked why he thought it might be for sale. He said Turner wanted to meet to discuss the possibility. When they met in a motel near the Atlanta airport, it was clear that they had been misled. Turner said that CNN was not for sale and that he did not need the networks. Nonetheless, he later made and attempt to acquire CBS by means of a leveraged buyout using junk bonds. The most significant aspect of this story was not covered by the press. Very simply, it is this: At a time when the major networks were considered by the press to be "dinosaurs", here was a major cable operator who, by his own actions, in contrast to his words, was ratifying the value of an established broadcasting network.

Whatever Turner recognized, anyone who understands the role of each of the three ingredients that networks manage (production, distribution, and funding) and analyzes the success of the Fox Network can argue that not only will the current networks survive, but more networks will be created.

The logic goes this way. In a field consisting of more than 35 channels of choice in a cable-equipped home, Fox provided a schedule of original entertainment programs for more than 180 independent television stations and joined them in a national identity. Until Fox, an independent station's program schedule consisted chiefly of off-network reruns, old movies, and perhaps some play-by-play sports. After Fox affiliation, the stations were no longer pure independents. Rather, they acquired a nationally recognized image, original programs, and industry stature. The sales success of the Fox affiliates in an otherwise soft market reflects that. The long-term success and viability of the Fox Network may still be an open question, but the fact remains that current affiliates are financially more successful than they were before affiliation. With Fox included, there are now about eight hundred stations affiliated with one of the four networks. This leaves about three hundred stations that can be considered to be pure independents. Since these stations have schedules that are predominantly comprised of reruns and old movies, as time goes by, it will become increasingly difficult to differentiate between an independent program schedule and a basic cable channel with similar programs. A nationally identifiable image may be their key to survival. This means displaying a common logo and carrying original programs as part of a common schedule.

Unless some owners of major groups of independent television stations undertake this kind of action, their stations may well fall victim to increased cable competition. It would be more than ironic if with the development of a changed media environment, the purely independent stations and not the networks turned out to be the dinosaurs of broadcast television.

We therefore believed that a fifth network would be created in the 1990s by a consortium of independent television stations in cooperation with one or more Hollywood studios. When we established this theory in 1992, we believed it would happen in 1994 or 1995, when the growth in cable penetration had almost stopped. Our theory was ratified in October of 1993, when a consortium of Chris-Craft Industries and Paramount Communications announced plans for a fifth television network to commence service in January of 1995. There was even further activity in this area by the Warner Brothers studio and the Tribune Company, owner of a group of independent television stations.

When the new networks were announced in the press, the articles listed station groups that agreed to carry the new programs. Included were companies that were already affiliated with a least one of the four older networks. This decision raises the issue of circulation. If the stations preempt certain programs of Network X in order to clear the programs of a new network, it will have a negative effect on total circulation, thereby causing a further erosion in the overall strength of the Network X. This appears to be a decision that could only have a longer-term detrimental impact on both the network and the local station.

Part of the motivation for studio-started networks stems from the belief that forming a network can provide a national outlet for programs produced by the studio.

While the concept of a fifth network can be supported by the more than three hundred stations that do not have a network affiliation, the odds against a sixth network achieving financial viability are quite high. The reason for that is the relationship between program production, distribution, and funding. All three areas must be sufficient in scope in order to attract a sizable audience. Here again we need to remember that the audience size is finite, as is funding, which is tied to the audience size.

While we can understand the objectives on the part of the creators of new networks, we also know that the conditions necessary for success are in very short supply, for reasons we have already discussed in other parts of this book.

Even though a shortage of remaining independent stations may make new networks less likely, the existing networks are prime properties for merging with a major production of organization. Who acquires whom doesn't matter.

The logic is simple. Despite all the hyperbole about their being dinosaurs, the three major networks and their affiliated stations still are the only means of reaching the whole country as well as its individual communities, and the only ones that offer a full menu of current live and original programs free of charge. No telephone bills. No monthly cable bill. No need for new wires or fiber optics. No dish to install. No cost for direct satellite transmission. The signal, the service, and the audience are already there, a known commodity with a record of half a century of community acceptance.

It is the history and performance that makes the ABC, NBC, and CBS networks primary companies to either acquire or be purchased by a major production facility. Rumors have existed since the beginning of the decade regarding the sale of NBC by GE, the acquisition of CBS by Disney, or the merging of ABC with Disney. Whether these, or any other permutation of them occurs by the mid-1990s, even their discussion ratifies the thesis of this book. This is why Ted Turner wanted to acquire CBS. It is why Larry Tisch did. It is why Capital Cities bought ABC. It is why Rupert Murdoch succeeded in creating Fox as a new network. Furthermore, the prospect of the acquisition and/or merger of a production company and a network has been enhanced by the elimination of the financial interest/syndication rules that were discussed in a previous chapter.

Having said that, we would also like to point out that there is a good deal of misunderstanding about the practical meaning of terms like *merging* and *converging* in this field. The linkage of a network and a major production source makes sense because both use essentially the same type of product, and because their distribution systems tend to be more complementary than competitive.

This is not always the case. During the last several years, many newspaper, magazine, and TV stories have talked about the "converging" of the television set and the computer. As we have pointed out, this may have more to do with the interests of the manufacturers than with the interests of the users. Neither the product nor the way it is used is common to both devices.

There have also been many articles about the merging of companies that have various businesses that appear to be compatible. The Warner/Time marriage is the most obvious example. Despite the Wall Street and other community excitement about the store of riches that are presumed to be realized by such developments, it should be noted, simple as it seems, that there is a major difference between merging and converging.

Mergers are important to Wall Street. Converging, if it is taken to mean the mutual enhancement of different businesses by putting them under one roof—a cross-fertilization (*synergy* is the preferred term) that makes the new whole greater than the old parts—is another matter. For that to mean anything, it has to show up in the living rooms of America. For Time and Warner to share a corporate home is one thing: for them to share a home screen is another. Mergers do not make words into pictures.

Or consider the following: just because Barbra Streisand has a contract with Sony Records, it does not mean that she will perform in a Sony motion picture for less money than that offered by Warner Brothers or any other competitor. Streisand would not like that. And neither would profit participants involved with any of her projects. And, either way, there is still only one Streisand. A merger does not expand the talent base. If it adds distribution, it only places more demand against the same supply of talent, which means higher costs.

As possible merger partners, the networks continue to be appealing to program producers because of their distribution strength. The capacity to reach more than 90 percent of America, as stated earlier, for better or worse, is only available on a consistent basis through traditional television networking systems. There is no new technology in existence or on the horizon—not DBS, not MDS (multipoint distribution system), not fiber optics, not cable, not CD's—that can match it. It is still the networks' trump card!

A network may find cable a useful outlet for some of its product—for instance, elements of sports events which cannot be accommodated in their entirety in the regular schedule, but whose rights and production costs have already been underwritten, or other, less costly events, not viewed widely enough to justify network exposure. This approach has been used by ABC, but the cable channel is clearly a secondary enterprise. On the other hand—as the short-lived CBS-QVC merger effort demonstrated—it is extremely appealing for a cable channel to gain access to a network's resources.

It is significant that the underlying feature of the various new business combinations in this field (those either being discussed or already achieved) is an effort to link the three fundamentals—production, distribution and funding—which were originally brought together in the network concept.

## Television and Society

We noted earlier, in "The Effect of Television on the Individual," that the micro effect of television—that is, its precise impact on the individual—is extremely difficult to gauge since every individual brings a different set of personal characteristics to the viewing experience. We were addressing then the tendency to impute to television an almost irresistible persuasiveness, subverting the individual will and the authority of traditional institutions and luring viewers into detrimental actions that they would not otherwise take. We do not think that that case has been made. There remains, nonetheless, the question of television's effects in the society at large—on the national and international scene—where collective responses to developments are concerned.

The most vivid examples arise from television's interfacing with extremely dramatic events in the real world—war in Iraq, famine in Somalia, genocide in Bosnia, slaughter in Tiannemen Square—under live or near-live circumstances.

It is obvious that this can lead to the kind of consciousness-raising that results in drastic action, but what is not so obvious is why this happens in some cases but not in others. Famine, civil or tribal warfare, and natural disasters are with us constantly and are widely reported. Sometimes the story takes hold and sometimes it does not. There are arguments over whether newsroom editors in America simply decide what is important and what is not, whether ethnic or cultural connections with the American audience is the key, whether the quality of the pictures is decisive, whether political or economic pressures at home (the"national interest") are the determinant, and so on.

It seems likely that all of these factors play some part in the process, but it is not easy to say which are the causes and which are the effects. It does appear that we have reached a point where it is difficult, if not impossible, to stage a quiet, unseen little coup d'état, hide brutal repression, conduct international terrorist activity, or undergo severe natural calamity, even in the most regressive societies, without the global eye taking note. Public life everywhere is more visible than it has ever been before. It is hard to see this as anything but an encouraging development. History tells us that repression and concealment have been collaborators in the past. Weakening that linkage may not lead to the dawn of a new age of civility and justice, but it is a step in the right direction. But, as we discuss later, with these benefits come as well, new responsibilities and new decisions for Americans.

## Violence, Television, and the Government

In May of 1993, a U. S. Senate Subcommittee on the Constitution held hearings with network and cable leaders on the issue of violence on television. The tenor of these sessions was summed up by Senator Paul Simon, who convened the hearings: "There are two choices: censorship or responsible voluntary conduct." To make this message more pointed, Senator Howard Metzenbaum reminded the broadcasters who were present that "they don't own the airwaves . . . they have a franchise. What Congress giveth, it can taketh away." This statement has overtones of the Newton Minow "vast wasteland" speech of 1961, but that is not unique. Such hearings have been held periodically for years. As far back as 1957, Senator Estes Kefauver included the subject of televised violence in hearings concerning a rising juvenile crime rate. Senator Metzenbaum's reference is to broadcasters' licenses. It is not clear what it signifies in relation to cable franchises, which are not granted in Washington, although the government can, and does, intervene in certain business aspects of cable as well. That is a form of indirect control. The explosive issue in these matters is not that kind of action, but a much more controversial one—content regulation.

Then, again in October of 1993, the Attorney General of the United States gave Congress approval to regulate the television medium if it did not do it itself. This action by the leading lawyer in the land succeeded in causing an increase in media attention to the topic, an increase in concern in the creative community, and an increase in tension between the networks, cable interests, and the Congress.

In reaction to all this, the four major networks promised

that they would reduce levels of violence in their programming and establish a system of labeling, so that viewers would be forewarned about content. Not mentioned was the fact that a much more far-reaching agreement on program, as well as commercial content, established and enforced for decades by the National Association of Broadcasters, had been struck down by the courts in 1977 as collusive.

In the precable, pre-VCR era, the NAB program code did affect the content on every television screen in the country. Today, with over half the homes receiving thirty or more channels, a network agreement certainly does not. To single out commercial broadcasters is at the least discriminatory, not to mention ineffectual. It is also interesting that the same Congress that has the greatest difficulty in imposing restrictions on access to instruments of real violence seems eager to support restrictions of fictional violence.

There are two ideas in contention here. One is a theory of social effects, widely and sincerely held, even if, in our opinion, imperfectly established. This is that violence on television leads to violence in life; that this is a social malady, and the government has a duty to protect the public from it. The other is an overriding principle of American government: freedom of speech. It is only in extreme cases of national interest—usually wars—that the protection afforded free speech is removed. Does concern about violence on television justify that sort of intervention?

If the answer is no, then the situation will stay where it has been for decades—lawmakers voicing concern, backed by generalized threats, and the entertainment industry listening intently and making equally vague promises not to go over some ill-defined line.

If the answer ever becomes yes, the real complications will set in. Some government-appointed body will have to start writing rules about how much violence and of what sort is allowable, and where and when. Ironically, that task will have a considerable legacy to draw on—the vast body of guidelines the networks have accumulated over the years attempting to accomplish a similar end. In those pages will be found speculation on such questions as what is allowable in a murder scene.

If a gun is used it has to be fired, and someone has to be hit. Should the impact of the bullet be shown? Should blood be shown? Should the wound be shown? How many shots and how many impacts can there be? If the wound and the blood and the impact are eliminated in the interest of non-violence, is it a serious misrepresentation of the effects of a deadly weapon or socially justifiable protection for the audience?

Those questions go on and on. And then those rules have to be implemented. Someone has to read scripts and look at film and decide whether a fictional post office massacre, based on a real-life occurrence, for example, is permissible, and under what conditions. There is also the question of whether the rules are to be the same for pay movies on television as for regular television fare. If televised violence does affect viewers, does it affect them more, or less, if they pay for it with services like HBO or rented videos?

How is the content delivered on home screens by pay movie services, rented videos, and commercial television stations made separate? Where is the line to be drawn regarding violence-heavy motion pictures? Because of the cost of producing action scenes, because of smaller budgets, products made for television contain less violence than theatrical films. Will motion pictures have to be edited for broadcasting over TV stations and basic cable but not for pay TV? Many are edited now for language and other actions deemed too excessive for broadcast TV. If the movies are to be altered for television, what is the point, after millions of people have already seen the full-fledged violence on theater screens? One reason the situation tends to stay where it is, is that both sides appear to be aware of these difficulties.

There is another aspect to this controversy that is not usually raised. As it is written, the First Amendment does not protect just good speech, responsible speech, wholesome speech, uplifting speech, intelligent speech, useful speech, fair-minded speech, accurate speech, socially redeeming speech, or any other category of speech. It simply protects speech. Good or bad. Period. And that is the only way it can work. Once the protection is subdivided, it ceases to exist, since the only way to enforce it is to have an official body make judgments as to which kind of speech deserves protection. That is what is known as censorship.

No matter what social benefits might be anticipated from government-imposed rules about violence or sex or any other aspect of television programming, assuming any system could be implemented uniformly across a one hundred-channel world, the mere fact of its existence would be a grave departure from our national traditions. We would have the government protecting the people from the presumed social effects of a specific form of speech that it has decided is harmful by preventing that speech from reaching them. It is impossible to say where this could lead.

It might be well to remember that the idea behind the First Amendment is not that all speech is good, but that obstructing speech is bad.

## Information and the Future

Another issue regarding new developments in technology is how the citizens of the only remaining superpower deal with the amount of disturbing news they receive about problems around the world.

Television in the 1990s, as we stated earlier, has made Americans witnesses to conditions that may have existed in obscurity for centuries but are now searingly real and immediate on their home screens.

Hunger and disease in sub-Saharan Africa is not new to explorers or missionaries. It is a new and highly emotional issue when brought into living rooms across America for the first time. As more developments in communications bring more information home to Americans, questions about responsibility, actions, and obligations become unavoidable: What should Americans do about the carnage of civil conflicts in foreign lands? Should America become the policeman of the world? Can America afford involvement? And what of Third World nations? What happens as technology creates a larger and larger gap between those nations that have it and those that do not, and at the same time makes that gap more and more apparent to both sides? Indeed, what are the potential consequences of the domestic version of this same inequity, when underprivleged Americans find themselves technological paupers? If technology-poor Third World nations find it harder and harder to compete, how do they ever address their social problems? What forces are unleashed as have-not nations become aware of progress made by the rich countries of the world?

Information and money can flow in two directions. Any progress, or lack of it, within any nation is known to all nations in this era of open communications

How the world deals with the flood of information unleashed by communication technology will unquestionably be among the biggest issues in the decades of the twenty-first century.

Regardless of what decisions are made, we do believe that if today's Third World nations are to develop as the rest of the world progresses, a free press will be a necessity. Without a free press, a true democracy is not possible. A government-controlled press is a tool of dictators and, as the world has already witnessed, ultimately ends in self-delusion.

## Quotes

The franchise on forecasts is open to everybody. As stated previously, most of the views expressed in this book are minority ones, at least in the sense that they are not widely shared in the industry. Since we were aware of that when we set out, we thought it would be enlightening to ask the opinions of a number of distinguished colleagues on the future of the industry. The question we put to them was this: How do you think most Americans will spend prime time ten years from now?

Here are their responses, which were not always limited to our specific question.

*Don Hewitt, Executive Producer,* 60 Minutes

Anyone who tells you he knows how Americans will spend prime time ten years from now is snowing you.

A good guess would be that football, baseball, hockey, tennis, and basketball fans will still be at the set but probably finding a charge on their phone bill for what they're watching.

Women, I would imagine, will be at the set shopping in department stores that may by the year 2003 have closed their retail outlets and moved their entire operations to "home shopping."

Kids who now go to the movies will be watching movies that come to them via pay-per-view . . . with some enterprising businessman having figured out how to deliver popcorn via cable.

In 2003, when there are two or three or four or five more channels for everyone than there is now, I imagine viewers will still complain: "There's nothing to watch on television."

If viewers ten years hence are still trying to find eight hours a day of worthwhile television fare, they're not going to find it then any more than they can find it now.

If they are content to get a reasonable return on what they paid for their TV set—a one thousand dollars a year or so's worth of enjoyment for the five-hundred-dollar TV set they're amortizing over ten years (that's fifty dollars a year), it'll be there. If they're looking for more than that, good luck to them. It won't be there in the next century any more than it was in this century. There aren't enough good showmen or good journalists to program all the new channels with stuff worth watching.

*Tom Murphy, Chairman, CapCities/ABC*

My best guess is that with the introduction of five hundred-channel cable, pay-per-view movies will be the major change in prime-time viewing ten years from now. I would guess that the networks would continue to have the lion's share of the viewing, but obviously less than they now enjoy. Pay-per-view movies would also cut into the audience of the presently established cable networks. All of this would lead to the software becoming more valuable. That is why it is imperative that the established networks have the opportunity to have ownership in the programming they now distribute.

I hope all indications are that the FCC is going to allow this to happen in the near future. If not, I am not as sanguine about the future of the established networks.

*Edward Bliss, Jr., author of biography of Edward R. Murrow*

On the subject of where television is headed, I do not feel competent to speak as to where the technology is taking us. But certainly, in this communications revolution, the changes will be sociological as well as technological. With multiplying sources, the audience is increasingly fragmented. As it is, we no longer have what Eric Sevareid called the "common hearth" provided by a few national networks. Not only will we be learning more and more about less and less, but in the sense that we no longer have facts in common, we no longer are one people.

The broker accessing more and more business news inevitably receives less information on foreign affairs, and the baseball buff, feasting on a sports channel, learns less about what is happening in Congress. My concern is that narrowcasting may lead to narrow minds. In any case, the revolution—the information explosion—will continue.

*Mike Wallace, correspondent,* 60 Minutes

How will most Americans spend prime time a decade hence?

This particular American will be underground with his toes turned up, so I don't worry excessively about it, but I have a hunch that ten years from now, despite what the crystal ball-gazers tell us, prime time will not be all that much different from right now.

Five hundred channels, so surely not as much broadcasting. Much more narrowcasting. Technological marvels will bring us hundreds of possibilities, we hear, including interactivity. Pay cable will be narrow, but it'll have to be a blockbuster to wean potential viewers away from all that will be available for free, or simply part of their cable fee.

I believe there will still be two major networks, neither of them NBC, with advertising-driven movies and dramas, comedy, and, yes, news, too. But it'll be stuff you'll be able to push a button for on your computer, whenever you want it during the evening.

The networks will still occasionally have the power to bind the nation together at one time, for live moments of high political drama, for disaster drama, wartime drama, for national celebration and national mourning.

All this variety will still be the stuff of prime time for most of us, I believe. And I'll wager that come 2003 at 7:00 p.m.—or whatever time you want to dial it up—*60 Minutes* will still be ticking for as many as fifty million Americans on Sunday nights.

*Walter Cronkite, former anchorman CBS Evening News and correspondent for various cable programs*

By the twenty-first century, television viewing will have undergone its greatest change since the invention of the tube.

The multiplicity of channels and the ability to call up programs on demand will have altered the entire concept of prime-time programming. Except for events coverage carried live, nearly all programming, including pay-per-view, will be placed in tape libraries to be recalled at the viewers' convenience. The concept of the nation sitting at home simultaneously watching its favorite program will be part of history.

Additionally, interactive programming will present highly visual and active games to be played in solitaire or by groups.

Family entertainment will take on a new dimension, which will also preempt some of that "prime time."

The networks probably will exist as program producers and marketers, but not in their present function as broadcasters of programs planned for simultaneous reception.

News, documentaries, and special events will be the province of independent organizations that may or may not have affiliations with the old network groups.

*Homer Lane, retired general manager, KOOL-TV, Phoenix*

There is little doubt in my mind that the structure of television will differ radically from what we know today. While programming will always be the dominant factor in television viewing, I believe that the networks of today will truly be the dinosaurs of the future. It is my opinion that the rapidly developing technology of fiber optics will permit home viewers to select whatever they want to watch at whatever time they choose to watch. There will be no need for networks, since whatever delivery system they subscribe to—cable, telephone company, direct satellite—they will be able to watch news and sports in real time and entertainment from an endless menu. There will be no need for a network in its present day form.

The television set will certainly be connected to an interactive system offering all sorts of services, some of which we cannot imagine today.

The local TV stations will be relegated to supplying local news as cut-ins on the various full-time news channels that will develop to compete with CNN.

All of this may result in the demise of TV advertising as a mass medium, capable of reaching most Americans for the introduction of new products and the marketing of national brands. The audience will be so fractured that the effectiveness of television advertising may well be severely limited. Perhaps we will see a resurgence of the mass circulation magazine as a prime advertising medium.

To specifically answer your question, how will most Americans spend prime time ten years from now? They will be watching their favorite movies, programs produced specifically for one

of the multitudinous program services that will exist . . .
watching news and sports in real time, and probably sipping a
Bud Lite.

The television set will be the centerpiece of a communications system that will combine and incorporate some of the functions of our computers, fax machines, video phones, etc. And
television programming will continue to be the centerpiece of
our mass culture.

*Bill Moyers, journalist, producer, author*

It's a ripe question, but I honestly don't know. We reporters
are better at telling you what's happening today than we are at
forecasting the future. I suspect there's something to the possibility that affluent folks will be able to "call up" any program
they choose at any time—"Dial a Choice"—but everyone else
will still be watching one of four or five "networks" even ad hoc
ones. But honestly, I don't know.

*Leonard Goldenson, former Chairman and CEO, ABC Inc.*

Of course, as you know, anybody's guess is good until technology takes certain leaps. I feel, however, that no matter what
the technology is, and I have always said this, whatever is on the
screen will prevail.

With respect to cable, I feel that if five hundred channels are
going to be available, cable will become more like radio, and
each cable network will have to direct itself to a specified
audience—or shall we call it narrowcasting?

With respect to the four television networks, and perhaps
one or two others as time goes on, as I said above, what is on the
screen is what is going to count. I definitely feel that there is
going to be a place in the future for at least two or three networks
that will cover the overall picture in entertainment, sports, news,
and possibly interchange with the public in whatever form television eventually develops into.

*Richard Wiley, former Chairman, Federal Communications
Commission*

Almost everyone anticipates that, through video compres-
sion techniques, DBS, or fiber-optic technologies, the average

household will receive a much larger number of channels. I expect also that digital transmission of broadcasting will eventuate, bringing with it such services as HDTV (offering higher-quality pictures, sound, and graphics), interactive features, and even nonvideo data services.

As a result of these changes in the nation's television infrastructure, Americans will have a much wider choice of video alternatives—and much more control over their own viewing schedules. Movies and other popular entertainment features will be available pretty much "on demand." Also, there should be a broader selection of programming aimed at specialized viewing audiences (in particular, sports events). Such narrowcasting inevitably will lead to increased fragmentation of the viewing audience (although the "nationwide audience" will still exist ten years from now).

I anticipate also that improved picture, sound, and graphics quality, coupled with interactivity, will make educational and other non-entertainment uses of video much more attractive. Through the use of advanced computer technologies, "distance learning" via video will give general audiences and students much more individual "feedback" than is now possible in a typical three hundred-seat lecture hall at a large university. At the same time, creative uses of graphics and full-motion video will make home learning (including professional and technical training) an appealing alternative to prime entertainment programming. These features will likely be supplemented by the availability of efficient mechanisms to receive high-quality print-outs of books and other literature in the house. In an economy that "feeds on information," attractive in-house educational alternatives will become an increasingly important contender for viewers' time and attention.

All of these developments may also have the effect of redefining "prime time" itself. With increases in scheduling flexibility, peak viewing hours may be determined, to some extent, by each individual viewer rather than strict adherence to uniform schedules that are prepackaged for nationwide consumption.

*Charles Crutchfield, former General Manager, WBT,
Charlotte, N.C.*

The prevalent opinion, voiced by a growing number of those
in the industry as well as a disgruntled public, is that free television is almost at the end of its existence. Any attempt to mark its
trajectory must be based on irrefutable data. The restlessness
and dissatisfactions reflect the attitudes and concepts of some of
those in power who lack a responsible and coherent philosophy
of constructive mass communication. The future image of television depends upon those whom the industry will empower to
meticulously and soberly examine the debilitating factors that
infect its critical condition. A comprehensive diagnosis of its
ailments must be made before a restorative prognosis and ther-
apy can be implemented. And it is an obvious fact that such
remedial measures must be instituted as soon as possible to effect
any recovery. Those in power simply must squeeze the sleaze out
of free TV. They must leave that form of "entertainment" to
HBO, Cinemax, and the movies, where the public may pay for it
or ignore it.

Suffice it to say no one can predict the plethora of technical
implementation that will have an impact, not only on the industry, but on every facet of human existence. The insidious catholi-
city of the computer will endow its user total autonomy. Electronic access will provide infinite avenues of gratification:
HDTV, holographic environments, three-dimensional "feelies"
to tempt and seduce the injudicious viewer. Therein lie some of
the dangers and challenges of an electronic wonderland. The
ramifications are mind-boggling. An electronic universe is in its
gestation stage—its power waiting to be used either by angels or
demons. Cable and satellites have almost obliterated the broadcast networks' raison d'être. Their demise is imminent. Unless
the industry purges itself of the poisons that inflict it along with
the corporate will to purify and revitalize itself, free TV, particularly network television, will be the precursor of a universal
renaissance.

After the toxins that infected it have been expelled, constructive priorities and consistent regimens of altruistic policies

will provide the impetus and energy to produce, with even greater power, programs to entertain as well as fascinate, elevate, and encourage. Quality and responsibility will be the wellspring to fuel every endeavor. A perpetual quest for enlightenment and excellence will characterize every undertaking. Anything that would endanger morality and refinement will find no voice. Ignoble and ignominious arts will receive no sympathy. Self-aggrandizing and patently biased philosophies will find no platform. You may say "But the public won't watch it." I dare the industry to try it!

Entertainment will be provided without the traits of exploitation and exhibitionism. Comedy will rely on wit and charm, rather than vulgarity and profanity. News will be scrupulously gathered, documented, and presented with dignity and impeccable fairness, sans cuteness and vapid chitchat. Sports will be downscaled and returned to the intercollegiate venues, where assiduous students will find athletic exercises commensurate with their schools' curricula. Sober, mature artists will be recruited to create programs of meritorious quality and viable commercial application. Celebrity will be bestowed on those who exemplify dignified and inspirational excellence; decadence and debauchery will be anathematized. The revitalized and purified philosophies and policies will reawaken the awareness that every great communicator is able to amuse or intrigue while concurrently entertaining, uplifting, and influencing the audience. Beauty, aspiration, and rectitude are universal tonics for the human spirit; twenty-first–century television will have to address and satisfy those basic needs of humanity.

Program content in the next century will reflect the capacities and integrity of its creators. The texture of the shows will be dictated by the technical capabilities available. The dictum *mens sans in corpore sano* must be the aegis of the new age of television. If it will commit itself to the criterion of excellence, a new age of enlightenment and ennoblement will be under-way. But the seeds of its growth must be planted *now*. There are no alternatives. The industry must rid itself of the excreta and detritus that now corrupt it. Corporate introspection coupled with dedicated commitment and zealous application of resuscitated ideals will see a once beautiful and powerful phoenix arise from the ashes of its defilement and emerge as a bright and inspirational power of which we can all be justly proud.

Free television was not intended to educate or save the world. Nor was it created to teach our young ways and means of destroying it. I know because I was a part of that fledgling industry.

*Newton Minow, former Chairman, Federal Communications Commission*

I believe there will be convergence of the technologies now used in telephones, computers, publishing, satellites, cable, movie studios, and television networks. Already we see tests of optical fiber demonstrating the future. In Montreal tonight, a home viewer watching the hockey game on television can use his remote control to order his own instant replay, order different camera angles—and become his own studio director. In Cerritos, California, a viewer today can participate in an experiment to summon any recorded show at any time, day or night; and he can stop it, rewind it, or fast forward it.

Here in New York City, Time Warner is building a two-way, interactive cable system with 150 channels. People will be able to order any movie or record album ever produced and see and hear it when they themselves want to see and hear it. We see four hundred- and five hundred-channel systems on the horizon, fragmenting viewership into smaller and smaller niches, and we need to remember that for all their presumed benefits, these developments undermine the simultaneous, shared national experiences that comprise the nation's social glue.

At the Annenberg Washington Program of Northwestern University, we are developing a blueprint for the future of optical fiber. As this new technological world unfolds, the risk remains of creating information overload without information substance of analysis, of more media with fewer messages, of tiny sound bites without large thoughts, of concentrating on pictures of dead bodies instead of thinking human beings. Henry Thoreau warned us more than 130 years ago: "We are in great haste to construct a magnetic telegraph from Maine to Texas; but Maine and Texas, it may be, have nothing important to communicate."

*Dan Rather, anchorman, CBS Evening News*

The "Prime Time" of the future will be whenever an individual viewer wants it to be—personally, for him or her.

Viewers will have numerous options to interact with their televisions. For example, when one wants to see the "CBS Evening News," or any part of it, one will simply dial it up. The same with any other program segment: entertainment, news, or educational (such as university courses or language classes).

Television will be combined with computer technology to a degree that is barely imaginable today, and it will be far more internationally oriented. One will be able to dial into not only any North American program, but also programs from around the world.

My guess is that television for educational purposes will be vastly expanded and much improved compared with today.

*Red Martin, owner, WCAX-TV, Burlington, Vt.*

I start from the observation that, through history, the majority look for a good story. Books, magazines, radio, and television are the descendants of the troubadour. In my view, the sudden decline in network audience was not the growth of cable, but the appearance of the videocassette. Suddenly the accumulated library of feature films (each of which is based on a story, however well told) became available, and VCR owners could watch what they wanted when they wanted where they wanted—without interruption.

The loss was most severe on Saturday night, and what has reversed the trend?—*Dr. Quinn, Medicine Woman,* a well-written, finely crafted story. Of course casting, direction, and production are important, but in the beginning was the Word.

Now how will the stories be delivered? By HDTV? By multimedia computers? By NTSC TV? Over the air? By fiber optics? DBS?

What about multimedia computers? I think it is safe to say

these will seriously compete with the current VCR in the very near future. A major advantage is that the program material comes on the video equivalent of the compact disc, and the technology for storing pictures is advancing so rapidly that feature-length programs on a single disk will probably be available only a couple of years away. At the same time, the definition of the digitally controlled image on a computer screen already equals and often exceeds HDTV quality.

It won't take much to add first-class audio and large monitors to personal computers. So the potential is there to replace the VCR. However, the limitation as an entertainment device is the capacity of the studios. How many releases do they produce annually in total? One hundred fifty? So, even if everyone had one, there would not be sufficient product to replace broadcast television in prime time.

Fiber optics will unquestionably replace copper and the phone line, so your house will have the capacity to carry full-motion video on several channels. However, even if so-called video dial tone replaces cable, where will the stories come from? Is it likely that consumers will accept a phone bill after watching the Super Bowl?

That brings me back to over-the-air broadcasting, NTSC, and the networks. For all the technology development, I defy anyone to construct a distribution system that equals a network and its affiliates in its ability to deliver an audience to the advertiser of a nationally distributed product.

The combination is a giant engine of commerce that is now an essential part of the warp and woof of our society. The need for it will not vanish, and it is difficult to see what could replace it.

Further, there is the question whether anything else could generate and focus the enormous sums we all know are required to produce the several thousand hours of prime-time programming that are consumed annually. Cable operators may dream of one hundred million subscribers at $100 annually, but the resulting $10 billion has to be spread over one hundred channels. No one of them would have the resources to hold the high ground in Hollywood as the networks do now. So long as they hold it, no challenger has any prospect of getting the services of the quite small pool of first-class talent required to compete.

For all these reasons, I do not expect a cable-dominated distribution system to replace the current network-affiliate system. Moreover, there is a cloud no bigger than a man's hand in the cable horizon. That is a system that cancels the ghosting in television pictures caused by so-called multipath reception. Particularly in urban areas, the television set receives signals that have been reflected from various obstacles. These arrive at different times (measured in millionths of a second), and, since each line of a TV picture takes about sixty-five millionths of a second to write, the result is a series of pictures displaced across the screen, a distracting feature.

Much of the basic appeal of cable is the ability to provide a substantially ghost-free and therefore much more pleasing picture. If this advantage is removed, one can confidently predict a substantial erosion of the cable audience—for the reason that cable systems routinely experience a 20 percent annual turnover. Customers don't pay, get mad, move, or otherwise temporarily defect. If, when this new technology is available in sets, the defecting customer finds he can receive a first-class picture from available stations with network programming (which constitutes some 70 percent of cable viewing), he may well decide to forgo CNN, ESPN, MTV, and the like.

Satellite broadcasting is a wild card. Currently there is a small niche of devoted subscribers, but it would be much smaller if the satellite program vendor were prohibited from rebroadcasting network signals, a problem I believe the new cable legislation addresses.

*Fred Silverman, President, Silverman-Hargrove Productions*
*(telephone interview)*

There will always be network TV—four or five over the air—and six to ten entertainment networks.

A dozen to 1½ dozen will be broad-based channels.

Ten or twelve companies will be programming for network TV.

Networks will sell a night to Paramount or Warner or General Foods.

Niche channels will be PPV interactive.

Fifth network of independent stations

Current networks have to adapt

Too bureaucratic

Changing mix to inexpensive reality shows

Too many people

NBC vulnerable in news—may merge with CNN

Children—Government will continue to be involved

Network survival is a matter of adapting.

*Harvey Shephard, former President, Warner Bros. TV (telephone interview)*

TV networks will do joint ventures with Hollywood Studios because of changes in FCC rules. If networks want a piece of syndication revenues, they may have to share with studios the advertising revenues derived from the original network run.

Some of these responses resemble positions expressed in many newspaper articles and technical publications, but for the most part they reflect personal experiences. In many cases, these are unidimensional due to very focused careers. This should not be surprising, since most people in most industries have career paths along specific functional areas of interest. It is rare when employees have an opportunity to gain significant experience in all facets of a business enterprise, such as production, finance, and marketing. As we have discussed throughout, it is this lack of a balanced mix of experience, knowledge, and understanding that will jeopardize many of the ventures along the electronic superhighways.

Nevertheless, the responses are informed forecasts by distinguished participants in the communications community of the way television may evolve.

## Conclusion

Throughout this book we have emphasized the importance
of the relationship between production, distribution, and
funding as the key to the success or failure of a television
enterprise. First in radio, and then in the early decades of
television, these three functions were linked in a continuous
process by the network-affiliate system. In that process, each
element had to support the other, and all three were ultimately
dependent on audience interests. So, they developed in response to demand, step by step. The output of that system is
still the driving force in the medium.

One of these three functions—distribution—began to undergo rapid expansion in the 1980s as cable entered the market. Now, newer technologies promise vastly greater growth in
distribution—up to five hundred channels—in the 1990s.

The two kinds of growth are different, however. Originally, cable grew by adding more and more homes. Its future
growth will come from adding more and more channels to the
same homes. The first kind of growth adds audiences; the
second subdivides them. Since the broad-based programming
that is still the medium's main attraction cannot be expanded
at the same rate at which new channels are added, the viability
of these new channels will depend upon the public's appetite
for more and more specialized fare concentrated against more
and more limited interests.

We believe that the networks and their affiliated stations
will continue to be the backbone of the medium, and that the
success of the Fox Network supports this thesis.
Since reaching as many people as often as possible will still be
the networks' role, we have also stressed the importance of
standards. If the networks try pushing the envelope in regard to
sex and violence, they will do so at their peril. They must be
welcomed into the nation's homes, day after day, night after

night. To do that, the networks must occupy a centrist position.

Finally, there is the issue of television as a subversive counterculture whose menace consists of its ease of use. The "television" America is the America that fought and won a forty-five year struggle against Communism, a vast and belligerent tyranny, without the bloodshed of a World War; that became the first nation ever to send a majority of its youth into higher education; placed a man on the moon; improved almost every measurable aspect of its standard of living; brought about outstanding developments in health, medicine, and science; perseveres in the enlargement of liberty at home; and remains today, a beacon to the world.

We do not see America's Class of '94, however one wishes to define it, as some sort of brain-damaged, culturally deprived version of the Class of '54, with which we emerged in the medium's infancy. If the claimed damages were real, surely it would be apparent in the leaders and the college students of this generation.

Whatever the critics may say, history seems to have rendered a judgment of its own on the impact of television in America.

# Postscript: A Failed Takeover Attempt

In 1985 a story that was making headlines was Ted Turner's attempt to take over CBS. This was one of the many speculative maneuvers set off by the FCC's elimination of the Trafficking Rule several years earlier. Turner proposed to make an offer backed by junk bonds to CBS shareholders. The offer never became active because it was rejected by the CBS Board of Directors. That decision was challenged in, and upheld by, the court.

That much is history, but a piece of the story survives in the form of a memo that outlines the reasons underlying CBS's rejection of the offer.

The memo is of interest as a rare, real-life illustration of the business principles by which the network operated—where the money came from, how it was invested, how the cycle of production, distribution, and funding actually worked, what the actual margins were, and what it took to maintain the stability of the system. The memo, in its entirety, follows on pp. 215–20.

## Appendix
## CBS Memorandum

FROM: Gene F. Jankowski
TO: WILLIAM LILLEY III
DATE: May 30, 1985

It is not feasible for a reduced CBS (no Radio and no WCAU-TV) to generate the additional pre-tax profit during the next six years needed to service the obligations to be incurred in the proposed TBS Exchange offer. In my judgment, the average annual growth in profit needed to service that debt would have to approach 18–20 percent versus the current projection of 8–9 percent growth as estimated by Wall Street analysts who are expert in following industry trends. An economic downturn, which our projection does not assume, would have even greater adverse consequences for such growth.

The CBS Television Network now is the acknowledged leader in both profit generation and cost containment; and we are very proud of that fact. While it always is possible to improve, and while we are working very hard to make continued improvements in both profits and cost containment, we feel strongly that we are performing optimally at this time.

In order to generate the drastic savings needed over the next six years, there are only three major areas from which substantial cost savings could come: first, and by far the largest, is programming; second is program development; third, and the smallest, is administrative overhead/personnel. It is impossible to see how substantial cost cuts in each of these areas would improve profitability; instead cuts of this size would significantly reduce profitability for reasons described below. Thus, efforts to achieve massive cuts would be self-defeating. Television profit growth evolves from ratings improvement and cost containment. Consider the following:

• A television network comprises four markets: advertisers, program suppliers, affiliates and audiences, none of which are directly controlled. Success in any of these markets depends on success in all of them. The best programming draws the strongest affiliates who bring the largest audiences who attract the most advertising revenues which enable a network to compete for the best programming. When managed well, the premiere network can maintain its leadership. If managed poorly, a weak member of this "chain" can cause further deterioration in all members. Drastic cost of the magnitude required by the TBS Exchange offer would change the relationshp among these four markets and would lead to rapid and significant deterioration.

• CBS is already the leader in Prime Time and Daytime which account for approximately 75 percent of television (Network and Station) and profit.

We are number one in Evening News and Sports. While our goal is to be number one in Late Night and Children's, a return to leadership in either daypart would not generate the needed cash. Increased ratings in any daypart are normally a function of well invested funds and therefore, increased costs. Should ratings fall by one point due to a radical cost shift, the impact on profitability in the dayparts would be as follows:

Approximate Loss in Millions

| 1986–1991 | Daypart | 1986 |
|---|---|---|
| $    612 | Evening (Homes) | $ 79 |
| 543 | Daytime (Homes)* | 70 |
| 178 | Late Night (Homes) | 23 |
| 43 | Children's (Ages 2–11) | 6 |
| 85 | Evening News (Homes) | 11 |
| 76 | Morning News (Homes) | 10 |
| 110 | NFL Football (Homes) | 14 |
| 59 | NBA Basketball (Homes) | 8 |
| $ 1,706 | Total Profit Loss | $ 221 |
| $    882 | *Daytime (Women 18–49) | $ 114 |

• Entertainment and Sports Programming: Virtually every broadcast makes a profit. While some program and talent fees have increased dramatically in recent years (e.g., NFL television rights), creating problems for profit growth, the network would still lose profit by canceling even the most expensive broadcast. It is enticing to speculate that our current quality programming, particularly our prime-time programming, could be replaced with low-cost, low-quality programming in order to maximize short-term cash flow. Such an action would clearly lead to lower sales, would result in lower affiliate clearances and thus lower ratings, and would cause the Network to enter a severe downward spiral in profitability.

Such irresponsible, shortsighted program cost reductions would eventually result in seriously reduced cash flow and would materially diminish the quality of programming presented to our audience.

Success of a network schedule requires strength in all program areas.

For example, if the merged broadcast operation were managed to maximize short-term cash flow to service excessive debt burden, then the operation would not have the residual resources to acquire expensive, long-term programming rights like NFL Football, which comes due for competitive bidding in 1986. Not only would cash flow be reduced by not renewing the NFL, since NFL makes money, but, more importantly, the lead-in to the Sunday prime-time schedule (the largest audience night of the week) would be ruined, seriously jeopardizing the evening schedule, resulting in losses of millions.

In addition, other dayparts would be affected by the loss of promotional time in the NFL. Finally, a stronger NFL schedule would emerge on one or both of the other networks, further lowering our ratings and profitability.

Another example of the new entity's inability to compete would be the Olympics. The cash-poor entity could not bid on this event, since significant ($50–$100 million a year) payments are required years before the event airs. The resulting duopoly network market could drastically affect Olympic coverage. One scenario might be that the other two networks agree to split Olympic coverage at lower costs to them and significant rating advantages for each of them and profit reduction to a restructured CBS.

• Program Development: A dangerous source of short-term profit improvement is a reduction in program development and advertising expenditures. Complete elimination of these expenses from

1986 to 1991 would not produce the necessary funds. Obviously, this elimination would have fatal consequences for profit. Experience teaches that even minor reductions in these expenses for short periods can seriously jeopardize profit. We did this once with disastrous results. CBS's fall from prime-time leadership in 1976–1977 followed reduced program development from 1973 to 1975.

It took three years to regain our audience levels. We were able to do this only through substantially increased development expenditures provided, in part, by cash generated by CBS's non-broadcast businesses.

During the next six years, CBS will need to introduce 50 to 60 new shows to prime time to replace aging shows. An elimination or serious reduction in program development would unquestionably result in a loss of audience and consequential loss of profit. The Network currently spends approximately $50 million per year in developing new shows. The "R&D" expenditure is absolutely essential to the continued success of this enterprise. Cutting this expenditure to maximize short-term cash would lead only to reduced profits—and in a very short time, as we saw in 1976–1977.

By way of further example, between 1977 and 1985 the entire Network prime-time schedule (except for *60 Minutes*) turned over; in other words, all shows now on the Network for the upcoming season were drawn from the approximately 220 pilots produced at a cost of about $250 million over the last eight seasons.

• Administrative Overhead/Personnel: Head count reductions are costly in the short run, seriously undermine employee morale, and are successful only when a change in business conditions (e.g., automation) warrant. Reducing head count simply to generate more cash could put CBS at a serious competitive disadvantage. CBS television costs are primarily program and talent fees. Administrative personnel costs are approximately 4 percent of total costs. Even decimating the overhead staff would not materially increase profit. It is my understanding that statements have been made, which I find most irresponsible, that overhead costs can be reduced substantially.

In fact, I have repeatedly heard reports from Wall Street analysts that it has been said that our costs can be reduced by several hundred million dollars. Since programming and development costs cannot, in my view, be substantially reduced without reducing sales and profits, I assume that they intend some substantial administrative personnel costs which, as I said above, are 4 percent of total costs and which, if cuts were to be made, would have to come at the expense of services directly related to on-air production. For example, our head count has grown only 5.9 percent from 1981 to 1984 (5,030 to 5,325) when our hours of programming have grown by 20.9 percent (5,173 to 6,252).

Moreover, the Wall Street analysts who follow us quite closely, and who are generally conceded to be expert, credit CBS with being the industry leader in cost containment ("Communications/Broadcasting," The Wall Street Transcript, April 29, 1985, pp. 77, 766–77).

Finally, the administrative personnel now employed in our operations are highly skilled, and many of them perform functions, such as market forecasting and pricing of network time, which directly contribute to market-share performance and resultant network profitability. For example, the loss of one percentage point in market share due to inexperienced management or insufficient management would reduce profits per year by the following amount by daypart:

Approximate Loss in Millions

| 1986–1991 | Daypart | 1986 |
|---|---|---|
| $ 263 | Evening | $ 34 |
| 119 | Daytime | 15 |
| 102 | Sports | 13 |
| 59 | News | 8 |
| 17 | Children's | 2 |
| 17 | Late Night | 2 |
| $ 577 | Total Profit Loss | $ 74 |

• As a result of the tremendously increased risk of a highly leveraged network, struggling to meet an excessive debt burden, the Network's cost and cash-flow requirements would increase, because talent and program suppliers would demand up-front and guaranteed fees, as a precondition of doing business. This network would be at a disadvantage when negotiating these fees versus a network whose long-term profitability is assured and who could afford to advertise, which is critical to the successful introduction of new talent and programming. Over time, the weakened program schedule, which inevitably flows from the above, would make CBS the last network a program supplier would approach, because of this greater risk. Being denied first choice would hurt our chances of introducing successful new programs.

Television profitability is ultimately a function of audience satisfaction as measured by ratings. Audience leadership in any daypart is the result of careful management of program inventory and scheduling. Conversion of that audience into profit results from cost control and sales maximization through commercial inventory management. Radical changes in program strategy usually result in <u>decreased</u> profitability. Increases in audiences are the result of gradual and careful changes, building on strengths and eliminating weaknesses.

Success in the television business stems from a seasoned team who carefully manage the intricacies of advertisers, program suppliers, affiliates, and audiences.

A financial condition which would compel a unilateral, abrupt, and radical change to <u>any</u> of these markets would cause a profit reduction. Once weakened, the fall in profit is precipitous. As the audiences depart, so quickly would follow affiliates and advertisers. Without the funding of other profitable businesses, as CBS had in 1977, the collapse of the business would ensue. the result of this "death spiral" would not only be a loss of network service in both its informational and entertainment aspects, but also a reduction in the market for all program suppliers, and the aftermarkets of independent stations, cable operators, VCR's, and equipment suppliers. Ultimately, the public would be the biggest loser.

*The following is the authors' commentary on the 1985 memorandum.*

By 1992, it was clear that the market did not grow at 18–20 percent; it did not even grow at 10 percent. The Turner bid fell through, but many organizations bought broadcasting properties during the period 1985–89, often with similarly optimistic expectations of market growth that would more than cover their heavy debt obligations. The trouble with this approach is that, while the market growth factor is flexible—it may go up or down—the debt obligation is not.

Gillett Holdings, Inc., filed for bankruptcy under Chapter 11; SCI filed; Tak Communications filed; Fairmont Communications filed. By the fall of 1992, there were at least a dozen other broadcasters hoping to stay out of bankruptcy. Also, a number of the banks and insurance companies that provided senior debt for media acquisitions have yet to see these investments provide the kind of return that was originally forecast. One large insurance company had over $2 billion invested in media companies, almost all of whom struggled to service their senior debt. In many of these cases, the equity and subordinated debt holders lost their entire investment. Billions of dollars have been lost because of poor forecasting. It is clear that if Ted Turner had acquired CBS on the original terms, millions would have been lost there as well.

# Glossary

**ABC**  One of three older networks programming to more than 200 stations. (Now CapCities/ABC)

*Ad Supported*  Programs that receive financial support from advertising and are free to the viewer. (Some cable programs include ads; so they are not always free.)

*A. C. Nielsen*  The Nielsen Television Index (NTI) provides estimates of in-home audiences of national television programs and is based upon a national sample of U.S. TV-equipped households, including Alaska and Hawaii. The NTI sample consists of approximately 4,000 metered television households. It is dispersed geographically to facilitate territorial and regional reporting. More 5,000 sample neighborhoods and sample housing units are selected for the NTI sample. As of January 1994, the sampling was based upon the 1990 U.S. census data.

Nielsen's meters are found in over 1,354 counties, which contain about 83 percent of all U.S. housing units.

*Affiliate* TV station that has contract to carry programs of one of the four networks.

*ATV* Advanced television. Technical System that provides more lines than current NTSC system, but not as many as HDTV.

*Barter* Method used by television station to acquire program by providing free advertising time in lieu of cash.

*CBS* Network originated by William Paley in 1927, now programming to more than 205 stations.

*CNBC* The cable channel owned by NBC; formerly FNN.

*CNN* Cable News Network.

*DBS* Direct broadcasting by satellite, enabling messages to be sent from anyplace in the world without the need for wired transmission.

*Electromagnetic* Range of frequencies that carry sound and
*Spectrum* picture.

*ESPN* Sports programming network owned by CapCities/ABC.

*FCC* Federal Communications Commission. Government agency created to manage utilization of electromagnetic spectrum and other communications issues.

*FNN* Financial News Network sold to NBC; now CNBC.

*FOX* The fourth-largest network, programming to approximately 184 stations.

*HBO* Home Box Office, a pay cable service.

*HDTV* High-definition television. New system provides sharper, clearer pictures on TV screen by using more lines when providing picture with 16:9 aspect ratio, rather than current 4:3 ratio.

*Interactive TV* A system whereby the viewer is able to react (talk back) to the programs on television with the aid of an hand-held electronic device.

*INTV* Independent television organization that promotes value of unaffiliated TV stations.

*MDS* Multipoint distribution system. Method of sending messages by microwave directly to homes.

*MSO* Multiple system operator—a cable company owning more than one system.

*NBC* Network owned by General Electric, programming to more than 200 affiliated stations.

*Network* Any number of stations carrying the same programming, at a common time, totaling 15 or more hours per week.

*NTSC* National Television System Committee formed by Radio Manufacturers Association in cooperation with the FCC in 1936. NTSC drew up standards for TV regarding number of channels, use of 525 lines of resolutions, and 30 frames per second. Such standards were adopted by the FCC in 1941.

*Pay-Per-View* Revenue-producing system whereby viewers pay to watch one specific event or program.

*PBS* Public Broadcasting System.

*Preemption* When a station or network replaces a regularly scheduled program with another one.

*Rating* Percentage of all U.S. television homes tuned to a specific program.

*RBOC* Regional Bell Operating Companies. Those companies resulting from breakup of old ATT.

*Share* Percentage of all of U.S. homes that are using television (HUT) at a given time tuned to a specific program.

*Subscriber* Home paying to receive cable services, though not necessarily watching its programs.

*Syndication* Programs sold or distributed by producer directly to individual TV stations, not using network distribution system.

*UHF* Ultra high frequency.

*VCR* Videocassette recorder, used to tape and play videos.

*VHF* Very high frequency.

*Viewers* Those actually watching a specific program.

# Bibliography

## Periodicals

*Wall Street Journal*   May 18, 1992   Cable Phone Link Promising Gamble [electronic superhighway]

*TV Guide*   Aug. 22–28, 1992   Is TV Violence Battering Our Kids? [TV violence]

*L.A. Times Magazine*   Nov. 15, 1992   King Stacks

*Broadcasting*   Dec. 21, 1992   Facts of the Affiliate Business [correlation, news profits]

*Washington Post*   Dec. 26, 1992   TV's Brave New World [500 channels]

Deloitte and Touche   1992 Monograph Series   User Perspectives on the Future of Wireless Communication [importance of mass market]

Time Warner   1992 Annual Report   The Future Is Now [electronic superhighway]

*New York Times*   Feb. 7, 1993   On a Clear Day, You Can Watch TV [TV and critics]

*Wall Street Journal* Feb. 9, 1993 GM Accuses NBC of Rigging [NBC/GM debacle]

*Broadcasting* Feb. 15, 1993 Top Execs Take Hard Look at TV's Future [Blame for Bland]

*Entertainment Weekly* Feb. 26, 1993 "Dateline" Disaster [NBC/GM]

*New York Times* March 4, 1993 An Uneasy Broadway Battles a Case of Spring Yawns [37 shows—6 stayed—creative failure]

*Broadcasting* March 8, 1993 Gartner Resigns, NBC Credibility Drops in Wake of Scandal [credibility]

*Electronic Media* March 8, 1993 Hubbord DBS to Carry Major Nets [DBS channels]

*Wall Street Journal* March 10, 1993 Loral Seeks Partner for Satellite TV [DBS]

*Daily Variety* March 12, 1993 Levis: Time to Rethink TV [electronic superhighway]

*New York Times* March 14, 1993 Tuned to Kids. She Takes Nickelodeon to Top [Kids' TV]

*New York Daily News* March 18, 1993 Jive at Five [Channel 4 sleaze]

*Broadcasting* March 22, 1993 Multiplexing and the Nets [500 channels]

*Wall Street Journal* March 26, 1993 Global Entertainment [rentals vs. box office]

*Broadcasting* March 29, 1993 Criticism of TV Violence Grows Back on Track [NBC credibility]

*Forbes ASAP* March 29, 1993 The New Rules of Wireless [wireless]

*New York Times*   March 1993   Silent Partner Emerging for Policy Counsels/TV [TV and attention]

*Broadcasting*   April 5, 1993   USA to Make TV Net Buy [cube—accepting ads from competitors]

*Washington Post*   April 6, 1993   The Video Vise [no secrets—world watchers]

*Washington Post*   April 6, 1993   Yes, Blame TV [TV violence]

*New York Times*   April 11, 1993   The Digital-Cellular-Video Revolution Is Running Late [merge of computer and TV screens]

*Forbes*   April 12, 1993   Encore? [movie production funding]

*Wall Street Journal*   April 12, 1993   The Not So Brave New World of TV [500 channels]

*New York Times*   April 18, 1993   News Magazines Step Up in the World [network erosion]

*Broadcasting*   April 19, 1993   Top 5 Basic Cable Service [ratings]

*New York Times*   May 9, 1993   At Leisure: America's Use of Downtime [TV usage by day of week]

*New York Times*   May 9, 1993   Why Cheers Proved So Intoxicating [importance of schedule]

*New York Review*   May 13, 1993   The Case Against Science [TV critics]

*Broadcasting*   May 24, 1993   SET's Kurnit Joins Prodigy [Merge TV and computing, TV industry to Senate, self-regulation, not legislation the answer to violence]

*New York Times* May 24, 1993 Cult Film Is a First on Internet

*New York Times*   May 24, 1993   Pay Per View Scales Back Ambitions for "Events" Shows

*New York Times*   May 25, 1993   Top Rivals Agree on Unified System for Advanced TV

Medianomics Newsletter   May 1993   Undermining the Market [American Psychological Assoc.—people believe TV]

*Vogue*   May 1993   Men in the News [evening news]

*New Yorker*   August 2, 1993   CNN FAces New Challenges

*PC Computing*   Sept. 1993   PC's and TV's: Do You Really Want to Run Apps with Vanna White?

*New York Times*   October 24, 1993   Views on the Information Superhighway

## Books

Barnouw, Erik. *The Image Empire.* New York: Oxford University Press, 1970.
———. *A Tower In Babel.* New York: Oxford University Press,
———. *The Golden Web.* New York: Oxford University Press,
Baxton, Frank, and Bill Owen. *The Big Broadcast.* New York: Avon, 1966.
Bellak, Robert N., et al. *The Good Society.* New York: Knopf, 1991.
Besen, Stanley, et al. *Misregulating Television.* Chicago: University of Chicago Press, 1984.
Bower, Robert T. *Television and the Public.* New York: Holt, Rinehart & Winston, 1973.
*Broadcasting and Cable Yearbook 1993.* Reed Publishing, 1993.
Brooks, Tim, and Earl Marsh. *The Complete Directory to Prime Time TV Shows.* New York: Ballantine, 1992.
Brown, Les. *Television: The Business Behind the Box.* New York: Harcourt Brace Jovanovich, 1971.
Cole, John, ed.*Television, the Book, and the Classroom.* Washington, D.C.: Library of Congress, 1978.

Compaine, Benjamin M. *Who Owns the media?* White Plains, N.Y.: Knowledge Industry Publications, 1979.

*Conversations with Eric Severeid.* Washington, D.C.: Public Affairs Press,

Friendly, Fred. *Due to Circumstances Beyond Our Control.* New York: Random House, 1967.

Gates, Gary Paul. *Air Time.* New York: Harper & Row, 1978.

Gilder, George. *Life After Television.* New York: W. W. Norton, 1992.

Harris, Jay S. *Television: The First 25 Years.* New York: Simon & Schuster, 1978.

Head, Sydney W. *Broadcasting in America.* Boston: Houghton Mifflin Co.,

Hewitt, Don. *Minute by Minute.* New York: Random House, 1985.

Kendrick, Alexander. *Prime Time: The Life of Edward R. Murrow.* Boston: Little, Brown, 1969.

Kennedy, Paul. *Preparing for the Twenty-First Century.* New York: Random House, 1993.

Klein, Gene, and David Fisher. *First Down and a Billion.* New York: William Morrow, 1987.

Labunski, Richard. *Libel and the First Amendment.* New Brunswick, N.J.: Transaction Books, 1987.

Mayer, Martin. *About Television.* New York: Harper & Row, 1972.

Metz, Robert. *CBS Reflections in a Bloodshot Eye.* Playboy Press, 1975.

O'Connor, John E., ed. *American History/American Television: Interpreting the Video Past.* New York: Frederick Ungar, 1983.

Paley, William S. *As It Happened.* Garden City, N.Y.: Doubleday, 1979.

Powell, Jon, T., and Wally Gain, Eds. *Public Interest and the Business of Broadcasting.* New York: Quorum Books, 1988.

"Quality Time: The Report of the Twentieth-Century Fund Task Force on Public Television." New York: The Twentieth-Century Fund Task Force, 1993.

Schramm, Wilbur. *The Process and Effects of Mass Communication.* Urbana, Ill.: University of Illinois Press, 1955.

——. *Responsibility in Mass Communication.* New York: Harper & Bros., 1957.

Seldes, Gilbert. *The Public Arts.* New York: Simon & Schuster, 1956.

Stanley, Robert, ed. *The Broadcast Industry.* Hastings House, 1975.

Steinberg, Charles S., ed. *Broadcasting: The Critical Challenger.* Hasting House, 1974.

Steiner, Gary A. *The People Look at Television: A Study of Audience Attitudes.* New York: Knopf, 1963.
Stone, Joseph, and Tim Yoh. *Prime Time and Misdemeanors.* New Brunswick, N.J.: Rutgers University Press, 1992.

# Index

Acknowledgments, ix–xi
Arts & Entertainment (A&E), 6, 168
advertising revenues, 67
Affiliate Advisory Board, 87, 88, 113
Alcoa Hour, 79
Alda, Alan, 33
American Media System and Its Com-
    mercial Content, The, 133
American Psychological Association, 146
*America's Funniest Home Videos*, 93
*America's Funniest People*, 93
American Movie Classics, 6
Armstrong Circle Theater, 79, 169
Asner, Ed, 41
Astaire, Fred, 33
Attorney General, 190

Bach, Johann, 157
Ball, Lucille, 33, 169
baseball, 62
basic cable, 194
BBC, 170, 173
Beethoven, Ludwig, 157
Benny, Jack, 12, 56, 61, 169
Bergen, Candace, 33
Berle, Milton, 130
Beverly Hills 90210, 33
Bill of Rights, 116
Billington, James, 132, 134

Bliss, Edward, 198
Bogart, Leo, 133, 134, 135, 136
*Bonanza*, 130
Boswell, James, 139
Bradley, Ed, 103, 114
Bristol Meyers, 44
Broadcast licensee, 126
Burns and Allen, 169

Cablevision, 66
Caesar, Sid, 169
*Cagney & Lacey*, 41, 42
*Camera Three,* 169
*Captain Kangaroo*, 169
CBC, 170
CBS Cable, 70, 71
*CBS Evening News*, 72
*CBS Morning News*, 72
CBS News Standards, 115, 116
CBS Reports, 169
CBS Television City, 114
CD, 190
censorship, 195
Charles, Glen, 160
*Cheers*, 29, 160
Chris-Craft, 187
Chrysler, 52
cigarette advertising, 106
*Civil War*, 175

clearance, 92
*Cloud Nine,* 29, 35, 37
clutter, 83
CNBC, 69
CNN, 6, 26, 69–72, 119, 185
Cohen, Alexander, 112
Colgate, 44
college football, 66
Collingwood, Charles, 114
commercials, 84
Communications Act of 1934, 107, 110, 116
Community Antenna Television (CATV), 6, 26, 45, 52, 64, 67, 73
computers, 178–80
Carolco Pictures, 65
*Cosby Show,* 95, 107, 160
Cosby, Bill, 29, 33, 178
cost-per-thousand, 79
Council of Churches, 40
Crisis in Public Broadcasting, The, 167
Croft, Steve, 103
Cronkite, Walter, 114, 199
Crutchfield, Charles, 203

*Dallas,* 170
*Dateline NBC,* 93
*Day One,* 93
Daytime, 72
DBS, 158, 190
Decoder, 143
demographics, 78–79, 114
deregulation, 117
Destination, 143
Dickenson, John, 180
Dictatorship of Numbers, 36–38, 46–47, 125, 130, 135
Discovery Channel, 6, 168–69
Disney Channel, 6, 39
Disney Corporation, 18, 188
documentaries, 101, 124

editorial control, 103
Educational Television, 174–75
Edwards, Douglas, 114
*Eight Is Enough,* 29
Electronic News Gathering (ENG), 165
elitism, 139

Encoder, 143
Equal Time Provision, 107, 110–11
ESPN, 6, 75
European Broadcasters Conference, 40
Evening News, 164

*Face the Nation,* 169
Fairmont Communications, 220
*FBI–Untold Stories,* 93
FCC (Federal Communications Commission), 18, 38, 47, 73, 88, 106–7, 112, 117, 125–26, 169, 175, 177, 179, 181, 213
Fetzer, John, 16–17
fiber optics, 158
Financial Interest and Syndication, 18, 106–7
Financial News Network (FNN), 6, 68–69
First Amendment, 102, 104–5, 194
FM, 177
Ford Motor Company, 44, 82
*48 Hours,* 93
Fowler, Mark, 117
Fox Television Network, 56, 61, 93, 95, 119, 186, 188, 210
free time proposal, 109–10
frequencies, 13
Fuchs, David, 100, 111

Gallop Poll, 180
Gannet Foundation Media Center, 133
General Electric College Bowl, 169
General Electric Theater, 79
General Electric, 68, 80, 188
General Foods, 51
General Motors, 44, 52, 116
Gilder, George, 178–80
Gillett Holdings, 220
Gleason, Jackie, 78, 130, 169
Gleick, James, 180
Godfrey, Arthur, 12
*Golden Girls,* 78
Goldenson, Leonard, 201
Goodlad, John, 136
Good Society, The, 130–33
Grand Rapids, 16
Grant, Lou, 40–42, 58

*Great Debates,* 124
Griffith, Andy, 78
group encoding, 143
*Gunsmoke,* 130

*Hallmark Hall of Fame,* 80, 169
HBO, 6, 64, 194
Hewitt, Don, 197
High Definition Television (HDTV), 118, 175–78
History Channel, 168
Home Shopping, 6
Honda, 52
Hope, Bob, 12
Hottelet, Richard C., 114
*How'd They Do That?,* 93

*I Witness Video,* 93
IBM, 44
*I'll Fly Away,* 173
*In the Heat of the Night,* 79
Individual decoding, 147
Information Superhighway, v
Interactive, 180
Inventory, 77, 109

Jankowski, Gene, vi, 11, 81, 85–86, 107–8, 112, 114, 215
Johnson & Johnson, 44
Johnson, Samuel, 139
Justice Department, 19, 106

Kansas City, 101
Katz, Oscar, 113
Kefauver, Estes, 192
Kelly Gene, 33
Kennedy School of Government, 108
Kennedy, John, 124–25
Kennedy, Ted, 111–12
KOOL-TV, 90
Kraft Music Hall, 79
Kuralt, Charles, 40, 114

*Lamp unto My Feet,* 39
Lansbury, Angela, 33, 94
Lane, Homer, 200
Lear, Norman, 29
Learning Channel, 6, 168

Lee, Carl, 16
Leonard, Bill, 40, 185
Lever Brothers, 44
Librarian of Congress, 132–33
licensing fee, 57
Lifetime, 6
Lilley, William, 215
Lindsay, John, 107–8
LL Bean, 163
*Look Up and Live,* 39
*Los Angeles Times,* 132
*Lucy,* 130

*M\*A\*S\*H,* 107
Martin, Dean, 56
Martin, Stuart "Red," 176, 206
Marx, Groucho, 169
*Matlock,* 79
McLuhan, Marshall, 181, 184
MDS, 190
*Meet the Press,* 169
Metzenbaum, Howard, 192
MGM, 114
Michigan State University, vi
Midler, Bette, 184
Minow, Newton, 125–30, 132–36, 192, 205
*Miracles and Other Wonders,* 93
Monopolistic preemption, 145
*Moore, Mary Tyler,* 58
Moyers, Bill, 201
MTV, 6
Mudd, Roger, 111
*Murder She Wrote,* 94–95
Murdock, Rupert, 7, 62, 188
Murphy Brown, 133, 163, 178
Murphy, Tom, 198
Murrow, Edward R, 116
must carry rule, 73, 76

National Association of Broadcasters (NAB), 119, 123, 137, 140, 193
National Football League (NFL), 33, 34, 59, 61–63, 89, 217
National Institute of Mental Health (NIMH), 140, 146
Nielsen, A. C., 54

Network affiliates, 26, 42, 47, 89, 91, 119
network compensation, 90–91
network erosion, 92
network season, 54
Neuman, W. Russell, 184
*New Yorker,* 184
*New York Times,* 46, 61, 180–81
*New York Times Magazine,* 20
News Hours, 93, 119
newspaper advertising, 85
Nickelodeon, 6, 39, 168
Nixon, Richard, 124

O'Connor, Carroll, 33, 78, 127
O'Connor, John, 127
Olympics, 65–66, 81, 217
*Oprah,* 133, 163
Orion Pictures, 42
Osgood, Charles, 40

Paley, William S., 87–88, 90
Paramount Communications, 187
Parr, Jack, 12
Pay Per View, 65–67
Pay TV, 52–53, 194
People Look at Television, The, 137
*PC Computing Magazine,* 180
Perdue, Frank, 86
*Playhouse 90,* 169
Poling, Harold "Red," 82
Prime Time Access Rule, 17, 92, 106–7, 160, 165
*Prime Time and Misdemeanors,* 124
*Prime Time Live,* 93
Prime time, 72, 106
Process & Effects of Mass Communications, The, 143, 149
Procter & Gamble, 44, 81–82
Promotional announcements, 84
Public Broadcasting System (PBS), 70, 169–75
"public interest, convenience and necessity," 117–18, 125
Public service, 117–18, 124–25, 127

quiz show scandal, 123
QVC, 6, 190

Radio and Television News Directors Association, 116
Rather, Dan, 114, 206
Reagan, Ronald, 117
Reasoner, Harry, 114
*Rescue 911,* 93
Rhoda, 58
Rubik's Cube, 47, 52–53

Safer, Morley, 103
satellites, 45
Scali, McCabe & Sloves, 86
scatter, 77
Schramm, Wilbur, 143, 149–50
Schwartzenegger, Arnold, 184
Section 315, 110, 112
Sellek, Tom, 33
Senate Subcommittee on the Constitution, 192
Sesame Street, 167
Sevareid, Eric, 115
Shakespeare, William, 157
Shatner, William, 33
Shepherd, Harvey, 209
Showtime, 6, 64
Shriner, Herb, 56
Silverman, Fred, 208
Simon, Paul, 192
Sinatra, Frank, 33
*$64,000 Challenge, The,* 123–24
*$64,000 Question, The,* 124
*60 Minutes,* 53, 84, 93–95, 103, 159–61, 163, 169, 175, 197, 218
Skelton, Red, 12, 78, 114–15, 169
Smale, John, 81
Sony Records, 189
Source, 143
Spectrum Fee, 172
Stahl, Leslie, 103
Stanton, Frank, 113
Star Theater, 79
Stewart, James, 33
Street Stories, 93
Streisand, Barbra, 189
Studio One, 79, 169
stuffing, 31
subscribers, 67–70
subscription fees, 172

Sullivan, Ed., 18, 78, 168
*Sunday Morning,* 40, 42
Super Bowl, 63
Sweeps, 54
syndicated programming, 20

Tak Communications, 220
TBS, 216
TCI, 65
technical standards, 176
telephone companies, 158
Television Audience Assessment Study, 140
Television and (Society, or Behavior?), 146
Texaco Hour, 79
Third World, 196
Time/Warner, 189
Tinker, Grant, 29
Tisch, Larry, 188
TNT, 6
Top Cops, 93
Trafficking Rule, 117, 214
Tribune Company, 187
Tufts University, 184
Turner, Ted, 185–86, 188, 213, 220–21
*TV Guide,* 115, 146
Twentieth Century Fund Task Force for Public Broadcasting, 166
*20/20,* 93
*Twenty One,* 124

UHF, 20, 177
Uncounted Enemy, The, 115
*Unsolved Mysteries,* 93
up-front, 77

*Upstairs, Downstairs,* 171
USA, 6
USC Graduate School of Education, 136
U.S. Steel Hour, 79, 169

"vast wasteland," 125–27, 131–32, 136, 155, 166–67, 192
VCR, 13, 19, 26, 45, 135, 155, 193
video rentals, 67
videocassettes, 20
videodisks, 20
violence, 193

Wall Street analysts, 189, 215, 218–19
*Wall Street Journal,* 65
Wall Street Transcript, The, 219
Wallace, Mike, 103, 114, 198
*Walt Disney Presents,* 169
Walters, Barbara, 101
Warner Brothers, 187, 189
WBT, 90
WCBS-TV, 85
Weather Channel, 6
Welk, Lawrence, 168
Welles, Orson, 15
Westinghouse, 71, 79
WHDH, 177
White, E. B., 127–28, 130, 133, 136
Wiley, Richard, 201
WKZO, 16–17
Wordsworth, William, 142
WTBS, 6
WTTW, 171
WWL, 90

Young People's Concerts, 169

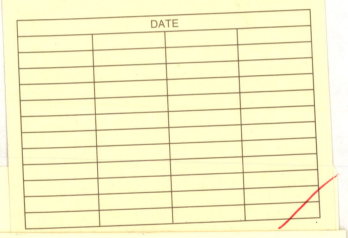

791.4509 Jankowski, Gene F.
J            Television today and
             tomorrow.

25100

**WITHDRAWN**

| DATE | | | |
|---|---|---|---|
| | | | |
| | | | |
| | | | |
| | | | |
| | | | |
| | | | |
| | | | |
| | | | |
| | | | |
| | | | |
| | | | |
| | | | |

y be kept

BAKER & TAYLOR